MEDIA LITERACY
Thinking Critically About
THE INTERNET

Peyton Paxson

WALCH PUBLISHING

1   2   3   4   5   6   7   8   9   10

ISBN 0-8251-4990-8

Copyright © 2004
Walch Publishing
P.O. Box 658 • Portland, Maine 04104-0658
walch.com

Printed in the United States of America

Contents

Media Literacy: The Internet

Contents

ACCORDING TO JEFFREY I. COLE, Director of the UCLA Center for Communication Policy and founder of the World Internet Project:

Understanding how people use the Internet is even more important than understanding the impact of television. While television is primarily about our leisure time, the Internet is already transforming work, school and play. Virtually every business, political and social activity will be affected by the Internet, and most activities will be dramatically transformed. Child rearing, consumer behavior, education, politics and religion are being changed dramatically by the Internet; these changes have unprecedented effects on our culture that need to be better understood.

This book, the fifth in a series that helps students develop critical-thinking skills through media literacy, focuses on the Internet. The guiding principle of this book is that the Internet can be used to teach critical-thinking skills. The units in this book provide students with information about the Internet as an entertainment medium, as a business, and as a source of social and cultural exchange. The activities require students to describe this new information and apply it in varied exercises. Students will analyze and evaluate how the Internet affects their lives and the lives of others. They will encounter ethical considerations and discuss issues of gender, age, and race. Students are also provided opportunities to use their own creativity and ideas in Internet applications. Ultimately, this book strives to make students more informed and more discerning Internet users.

The Internet's rapid diffusion and its sharply escalating impact on society make it difficult to assemble materials about the Internet that do not quickly become dated. With this in mind, an effort has been made to develop activities in this book that focus on "big picture" aspects of the Internet rather than current fads and short-lived phenomena.

To the Student

THE FEDERAL COMMUNICATION COMMISSION recently found that "Seventy-two percent of Americans are now on-line and spend an average of nine hours weekly on the Internet." This book presumes that you have some familiarity with the Internet, and that some readers are "power users." Many of you are probably the most knowledgeable users of the Internet in your home. If you already know a lot about the Internet, this book will challenge you instead of insult your intelligence. If you do not know as much about the Internet as you would like, this book will help you explore and learn.

Many of the activities in this book require you to use the Internet to find information. The best way to begin looking for information on the Internet is to start with a **search engine.** The following are just a few of the more useful search engines available:

- Alfa Seek   www.alfaseek.com
- Ask Jeeves   www.ask.com
- Alta Vista   www.altavista.com
- Excite   www.excite.com
- Google   www.google.com

Search engines typically use Boolean logic. George Boole (1815–1864) was a British mathematician and logician whose work has been used to develop patterns to search for information on the Internet. The four most common operators (symbols or words) used in a Boolean search are as follows:

+ Using this symbol between search terms will take you only to those web sites that contain all of those words. For example, typing Cleveland +LeBron +James at a search engine will create a list of web sites that contain all those words.

− Using this symbol allows you to look for web sites that contain a word or phrase but not another. For example, typing Cleveland − LeBron will create a list of web sites than contain the word Cleveland but not LeBron James.

OR Using this word will find sites that have any of two or more words. For example, typing Cleveland OR LeBron OR basketball will find all the sites that have one or more of those words.

"" Placing a phrase or sentence within quotation marks will take you only to sites where those words appear exactly as quoted. For example, typing "LeBron James' Nike contract" will create a list of web sites where that exact phrase appears.

There are probably several words in this book with which you are not familiar. You will find a glossary at the back of the book. Words that are defined in the glossary are highlighted in bold when used in the book.

The objectives of this unit are to help students

- appreciate the historical context of the Internet
- anticipate Internet-driven changes in the future
- understand that technological change has an impact on social and economic change
- recognize that technological change is constant and accelerating.

MOST STUDENTS TODAY realize that the Internet is of great utility to them. This unit is designed to help students place the Internet in historical context and begin to investigate the social, economic, and technological reasons the Internet came into existence. Students will also investigate the purposes the Internet serves, both currently and in the future, for a variety of users.

In this Unit. . .

Is Internet a Proper Noun? has students investigate how language-usage rules arise and are altered.

Computers Everywhere, in Everything encourages students to use creative thinking in identifying new applications and locations for Internet connections.

The Flexible Monitor introduces students to the practice of ergonomic design, and asks students to anticipate future uses of ergonomically designed computer screens.

Lost Languages has students evaluate the Internet's contribution to the loss of many of the world's languages during the next century.

Neologisms discusses how the Internet has led to the introduction of new words in English. Students then generate definitions for Internet-related neologisms.

Beaver College Versus the Internet uses a case study of how the Internet caused complications for an American college, and has students engage in creative problem solving to fashion a response.

Distance Education has students evaluate the advantages and disadvantages of using distance technology in education.

Technological Unemployment encourages critical thinking by asking students to assess the social benefits as well as the social costs of the Internet.

Viruses asks students to investigate the political, personal, and economic agendas that contribute to the creation of computer viruses.

The Changing Concept of Privacy has students explore the Internet's impact on personal privacy. Students also examine the social norms that contribute to the concept of privacy.

Cyber Crime provides students with information about several illegal practices currently being conducted on the Internet. Students investigate ways of preventing themselves and others from being victimized.

Will the Internet Become a Necessity? invites students to estimate the significance of the Internet in the future.

Internet Buzz

THE DEVELOPMENT of what we now call the Internet began in the United States in 1965. The United States Defense Department's Advanced Research Project Agency (ARPA) built a small network called ARPANET. The agency wanted to allow researchers at universities and other institutions to be able to communicate about the work they were doing for the government. The network began when four universities connected their supercomputers through a network in 1969. By 1971, more than twenty universities and government research centers were on-line. Two years later, the network expanded to research centers in Europe. It soon became clear that the most popular use of the network was e-mail.

By the late 1970s, ARPANET developers began to look beyond military applications for the network. The term *Internet* was used for the first time in 1982. The following year, the Domain Name System went into effect. Instead of trying to remember a web site address that had a long number, as had been the practice, a user only had to remember an address, such as www.walch.com. In 1990, the ARPANET network went out of existence. Two important changes occurred in 1991. First, commercial use of the Internet was allowed. Before, the Internet's use had been restricted to educational and governmental institutions. The second important development in 1991 was the introduction of the World Wide Web, which made getting information on the Internet much easier.

> **"The term Internet was used for the first time in 1982."**

Mosaic, which allowed us to see photographs and other graphic items on the Internet, became available in 1993. Of course, with graphics came banner ads. The first banner ads appeared on hotwired.com in October 1994. They were for Zima, an alcoholic beverage, and AT&T. Another use of graphic technology has been on-line pornography. Congress passed a law in 1996, the Communications Decency Act, that tried to prohibit distribution of obscene material over the Internet. However, the Supreme Court unanimously ruled most of the law unconstitutional the following year. In 2003, however, the Supreme Court approved a federal law that requires many public libraries to prohibit access to pornographic sites.

In 2003, there were nearly 30 million domain names, or web sites, in use in the world. Most of these sites used ".com" in their domain name. More than half of the world's web sites originate in the United States, and nearly three quarters of the world's web sites are in English. Today, the four parts of the Internet that most users are familiar with are the World Wide Web (for surfing), Usenet (for newsgroups), Internet Relay Chat (IRC—for live chat), and e-mail. These are not the only elements of the Internet, however, and other Internet channels will likely arise in the future.

Is Internet a Proper Noun? -

PROPER NOUNS are the names of particular people and their titles, places, dates, and events. For example, "Dwayne Washington" is a proper noun, as are "Omaha, Nebraska" and "Memorial Day." Current usage, as reflected in the spell-checker in most computerized word-processing programs, says that the word *Internet* is a proper noun that should be capitalized. However, other communication media, such as television and telephone, are not proper nouns. Some computer users distinguish an "internet," which is any collection of networked computers, from the "Internet," which is the worldwide connection of computers on which we can find the World Wide Web. According to this distinction, then, the Internet is the biggest example of an internet. Got it?

Rules of capitalization become rules when they gain popular acceptance. Rules of capitalization also vary from language to language. For example, in English, the names of languages are capitalized. In Spanish, they are not. Therefore, in English, we type the name of the language as "Spanish." In Spanish, we type the name of the language as "español."

Many people who frequently engage in instant messaging or Internet chat do not use capitalization. This includes the capitalization of proper nouns and the capitalization of the words at the beginning of sentences.

Record your answers below. Use another sheet of paper, if necessary.

1. Why do you think that rules of capitalization were invented in the first place?

2. Do we still need capitalization today? Why or why not?

3. Regardless of how you answered question 2, what would be an advantage of doing away with capitalization?

4. Regardless of how you answered question 2, what would be a disadvantage of doing away with capitalization?

5. Do you think that as people use computers more frequently to communicate that the use of capitalization may someday end altogether? Explain why or why not.

Computers Everywhere, in Everything - - - - - - - - - - - - - - - -

BILL GATES, Microsoft's chairman, wrote in an essay entitled "The World in 2003" that,

> Computers are becoming smaller, more powerful, less power-hungry and far less expensive, making it easier to build computing power and connectivity into everyday devices. . . . this will lead to a fundamental change in the way we perceive computers. Using one will become like using electricity when you turn on a light. Computers, like electricity, will play a role in almost everything you do in the future . . .

If you agree with Gates, it may not surprise you that LG Electronics, a Korean company, now makes an Internet Refrigerator. (You can check it out at www.lgappliances.com.) This refrigerator, available in the United States, has a computer monitor built into its door. Besides keeping food cold, the refrigerator allows users to send and receive e-mail and surf the Web. Whirlpool is experimenting with an Internet hookup that would allow people to "talk" to its Polara Range. The Polara is a combination cooking range-refrigerator. The on-line connection would allow people to use the Internet to tell the Polara to start dinner.

Okay, so somebody has already beaten you to a combination refrigerator-Internet browser and a combination stove-Internet browser. However, you could place a computer for Internet access within many other objects. (Use your imagination!) List three objects below, and explain why each would be a good idea for adding Internet connectivity:

1.

2.

3.

The Flexible Monitor- -

ERGONOMICS, also called human engineering, is the science that tries to arrange and design things so that people can use them safely and efficiently. For example, the computer mouse is designed to fit easily and comfortably within the average person's hand. A computer desk is designed to allow the user to type on the computer's keyboard at a comfortable height while seated.

Engineers have already invented computer screens that are thin, flexible, and foldable, like paper. These screens can be the size of current computer monitors, as small as a credit card, or as large as a kitchen table. One of the next challenges for the engineers is to make these new computer monitors affordable for the average computer user. Another challenge for the companies that will sell these paperlike computer monitors is to make people want them.

Record your answers below. Use another sheet of paper, if necessary.

1. List and describe three uses that product manufacturers will find for paperlike computer monitors.

   •
   •
   •

2. List and describe three reasons why you think people will want to buy paperlike computer monitors when they become available to consumers.

   •
   •
   •

3. Would you want a paperlike computer monitor? Explain why or why not.

4. Do you think that paperlike computer monitors will eventually completely replace the current types of computer monitors? Explain why or why not.

Lost Languages -

MICROSOFT, the world's largest computer **software** company, developed Internet Explorer, the most commonly used Internet browser. Microsoft makes software in at least thirty languages. That may sound like a lot. However, there are about 6,800 languages used in the world today.

Linguists (the people who study languages) predict that about half of those 6,800 languages may be lost during the next century.

How does a language get lost? The group of people who speaks a language gets smaller and smaller. This happens as the children of the group are educated in another language, watch television and see movies in another language, and read magazines and newspapers in another language. The United Nations Educational, Scientific and Cultural Organization (UNESCO) estimates that 3,500 to 4,000 of the world's languages no longer have speakers who are children. Eventually, the older people who still speak the original language die, and their language dies with them.

Hundreds of Native American languages have been lost since Europeans began arriving in the western hemisphere in the 1400s. Part of this loss was due to United States laws that forbid the teaching of Native American languages in schools. These laws are no longer in effect, and many Native American groups are working to preserve their native tongues.

Despite efforts by some to keep dying languages alive, linguists estimate that half the people on the planet use only fifteen languages to communicate. They also estimate that half of the 6,800 existing languages are spoken by less than ten percent of the world's population.

It is estimated that more than a third of all the web sites on the Internet appear in English. This does not mean that English will become the world's only language. In fact, the percentage of English-language web sites on the Internet is declining as web sites in other languages become more common. However, some linguists believe that the fact that there are few or no web sites available in hundreds, even thousands of languages may contribute to the gradual death of those languages.

Answer the following questions. Use another sheet of paper, if necessary.

1. Why do you think that linguists believe that the Internet will help the spread of some languages, while contributing to the loss of other languages? Explain your answer.

(continued)

Lost Languages -

2. If we will still have thousands of languages in the world, should we care that some languages are dying? Explain why or why not.

3. What else is lost when a language dies? Explain your answer.

4. Why do you think that it was once illegal to teach Native American languages in United States schools?

5. Why do you think that the United States got rid of the laws that forbid the teaching of Native American languages?

6. There is currently a movement in the state of Hawai'i to preserve the Hawaiian language. (In fact, using the apostrophe in the state's name is part of an effort to represent more accurately the state's Hawaiian name.) The organizations that are helping Hawaiians learn the native language receive taxpayers' support. Imagine that you live in Hawai'i. Do you think it would be a good idea or a bad idea to use some of your taxes to pay to teach people the Hawaiian language? Explain your answer.

Neologisms -

ALTHOUGH THE INTERNET may contribute to the death of some older languages, it is also responsible for the creation of new words. The formal term for a new word is *neologism*. Some neologisms are not truly neologisms, but new uses of old words. For example, the word *gay* today has different meanings than it did 100 years ago. Some neologisms are the result of combining existing words. For example, a *wannabe* is a person who wants to be something he or she is not. Some words originate as slang among teenagers. *Phat* is now in the Merriam-Webster dictionary, but it is probably best to be careful when telling an older adult that they are *phat*.

The Internet and computers have proved to be a great source of neologisms. Sometimes this is a problem. As discussed in Activity 10 in this unit, the verb *google* (lowercase g) means to use the search engine www.google.com to look something up. Google (capital G), the company that owns www.google.com, is worried that its trademark could become a common word. For example, the word *aspirin* was once a trademarked word owned by Bayer. It has since become a generic or common word, and Bayer has lost its legal right to exclusive use of the word. Understandably, then, the Xerox Corporation does not want us to the use the verb *xerox* when we mean the verb *photocopy*.

Suppose that Ancient Andy was frozen in a block of ice for the past ten years. He was recently rescued and has thawed out. Andy needs you to describe some of the neologisms that have arisen from the Internet while he was frozen. Since Andy has not been around for awhile, make certain that you do not use other neologisms when defining the following neologisms for him.

(Write your definitions. It is not fair to use dictionaries, the Internet, or other sources to help you!)

1. netiquette—

2. blog—

(continued)

Neologisms -

3. spam—

• Who do you think is worried about the use of the word *spam* (with a lowercase s)?

4. search engine—

5. flame—

6. download—

7. cyberspace—

8. hit—

9. login—

10. virus—

Beaver College Versus the Internet -----------------

BEAVER COLLEGE and Musical Institute was established in 1853 in Beaver County, in western Pennsylvania. The school later moved across the state to Glenside, a suburb of Philadelphia. The school was founded as an all-women's school, but later became coeducational, admitting male students. Thousands of students have graduated from the school and have its name on their diplomas. Within college circles, Beaver College had a good reputation, and students, teachers, and graduates of the college were understandably proud.

You may already know that "beaver" is a vulgar slang expression. Because of this, media personalities, such as David Letterman and Howard Stern, referred to Beaver College in jokes on their programs. Research by the college found that nearly thirty percent of the high school students it surveyed were not interested in applying to the college because of its name alone. As a result, there were discussions about changing the school's name.

Record your answers below. Use another sheet of paper, if necessary.

1. From the facts above, list three reasons why some people associated with Beaver College wanted to keep the school's name.

    •

    •

    •

2. From the facts above, list three reasons why Beaver College considered changing its name.

    •

    •

    •

(continued)

Beaver College Versus the Internet - - - - - - - - - - - - - -

3. Imagine that you are already a student at Beaver College. The school is discussing changing its name. Would you want the school to change its name or not? Explain your answer.

An additional issue that Beaver College faced concerned the Internet. Many Internet users have filters on their e-mail that screen out e-mail with vulgar language. There is also filtering software that will not allow users to go to certain World Wide Web sites where vulgar language appears. As a result, some Internet users who were seeking information about different colleges could not access Beaver College's information. Also, some Internet users who did not use filtering software accidentally visited web sites where vulgar words and images appeared while looking for Beaver College's web site.

4. If you worked for Beaver College, what would you do to help students access information about the school on the Internet? Explain your answer.

5. What did the college decide to do? Conduct an Internet search, and find out. Describe what you found.

Distance Education -

DISTANCE EDUCATION uses Internet technology to educate students in a variety of settings. For example, Indiana University (www.indiana.edu) offers over 100 high school courses on-line. Depending on a student's needs, he or she can enroll in just a few courses, or can take all of their high school courses on-line, and earn their high school diploma without ever leaving home.

Many colleges in the United States today also offer courses through distance education. Some colleges offer entire undergraduate and graduate degree programs on-line. There is even an on-line law school, Concord Law School (www.concordlawschool.com).

Many distance education courses are *asynchronous,* which means that the students in a course do not all have to be on-line at the same time. For example, a class may have a Friday deadline to complete a project. Julie can work on her project on-line on Tuesday morning and Wednesday evening. Li may work on his project on Thursday afternoon. Because courses can be taken asynchronously, it does not matter where you live. Students enrolled in the same course can live in California, in New Jersey, or even in Kenya or Thailand. For example, Southern New Hampshire University (www.snhu.edu), which has its main campus in Manchester, New Hampshire, has distance education students in all fifty states and in twenty-three time zones around the world.

Record your answers below. Use another sheet of paper, if necessary.

1. Think about your schooling. Would you be interested in taking some or all of your classes through distance education, or none at all? Explain your answer.

2. List what you think would be three advantages of earning a high school diploma or college degree through distance education. Explain each.

   •

   •

   •

(continued)

Distance Education –

3. List two types of people that you think would be the most interested in distance education. Explain both.

    •

    •

4. List what you think would be three disadvantages of earning a high school diploma or college degree through distance education. Explain each.

    •

    •

    •

Technological Unemployment -

WE OFTEN HAVE TO UNDERTAKE a cost-benefit analysis when making decisions in life. Sometimes the decision involves an economic cost. For example, if you spend your money on a new MP3 player, you will not have that money to go out to see a movie. You must weigh the benefit of the MP3 player against its economic cost.

Sometimes, we speak of an *opportunity cost*. For example, going to a concert with one group of friends may mean missing the opportunity to go with other friends to a party that same evening. You must weigh the benefit of going to the concert against the lost opportunity of going to the party.

When new technology is invented, it often helps create new jobs. For example, soon after the automobile was invented, the automobile industry became one of the largest employers in the United States. The demand for automobiles also created jobs in the petroleum industry. However, when new technology is invented, it often puts some people out of work. This is called *technological unemployment*. Consider what the invention of the automobile meant to the people who raised and sold horses for a living.

The Internet has caused, and will continue to cause, technological unemployment. For example, some bookstores have closed because they cannot compete with Amazon.com's prices. The people who worked at those closed bookstores lost their jobs. Many music stores have closed due to our ability to download music from the Internet. Some newspapers are laying off employees because people are now using the Internet to find information for which they once bought newspapers.

Record your answers below. Use another sheet of paper, if necessary.

1. List and describe two of the *economic costs* of the Internet.

2. List and describe two of the *economic benefits* of the Internet.

(continued)

Technological Unemployment -

3. List and describe one *opportunity cost* of the Internet.

4. List and describe one *opportunity benefit* of the Internet.

5. Do you think that the benefits that society receives from the Internet outweigh the economic and opportunity costs of the Internet? Explain why or why not.

6. Because the Internet causes technological unemployment, does that make the Internet a bad thing? Explain why or why not.

Viruses ---

A COMPUTER VIRUS can be described as a program, or computer code in a program, that makes a copy of itself, thereby infecting parts of an operating system (such as Windows) or an application program (such as WordPerfect). Computer expert Fred Cohen is credited with popularizing this use of the word *virus* in the early 1980s. Computer viruses have existed almost since the beginning of electronic computing in the late 1940s. However, before computers became widely networked, most viruses did not spread very far.

One of the first viruses to spread from one user's computer to others was one that affected Apple computers beginning in 1981. The first virus to spread through a Microsoft operating system was the Brain virus, which made its unwelcome appearance in 1986. By August 2003, nearly 65,000 computer viruses had been identified. More viruses are created every day. Not all viruses are *malicious* (meant to do harm). However, many viruses are indeed malicious and often highly effective at harming other people's ability to use their computers.

Why do some people create viruses? So many viruses have been created by so many different people that a single answer is probably not helpful. Here are some of the reasons cited: It is simply part of a person's personality; to be cool; to become famous; to make money; or for revenge.

Record your answers below. Use another sheet of paper, if necessary.

1. Why do you think people create computer viruses? You can refer to the list above or add your own reasons. List three reasons in order of what you believe their ranking to be—from the most common reason to the third most common reason. Next to each, explain why you ranked them as you did.

In the 1800s, many people were afraid that new manufacturing technology would put people out of work. This phenomenon, called *technological unemployment,* is discussed in Activity 8 in this unit. One group of people in Britain, led by Ned Ludd, broke into factories and smashed the machinery. Since that time, some people who oppose technology have been labeled Luddites. Today, some people, sometimes called neo-Luddites, have been vocal in their opposition to the growing emphasis on computers and the Internet in modern life. Most neo-Luddites have not

(continued)

Viruses -

committed any crimes in their battle against technology. However, as the original Luddites did, a small number of people within the neo-Luddite movement have resorted to criminal activity. Perhaps the most infamous neo-Luddite to resort to criminal activity is Theodore Kaczynski, the so-called "Unabomber." Kaczynski is currently serving life in prison for admitting guilt in bombings that killed three people and injured twenty-nine others.

2. Some of those who study computer viruses believe that some viruses are created by neo-Luddites. Ironically, people with the technological ability to create computer viruses may actually be opposed to society's increasing reliance on computers. Explain why you think some computer viruses may be created by neo-Luddites.

When a particularly nasty computer virus hits, some companies that rely on the Internet to earn money can be shut down for a period of a few minutes up to several days. Of course, these companies know of that risk, and guard against it. However, one must consider just how much risk to avoid and how much to accept.

3. Suppose that you work for a company that relies on the Internet to make money. Consider the following information:

   • You know that there is a possibility that a virus could shut down the company, costing the company up to one million dollars ($1,000,000). There is no way of knowing how likely this possibility is. In other words, there may be a ten percent chance of a virus shutting down the company, or there may be a ninety percent chance.

   • Security equipment and software to fight viruses cost $50,000. The basic system will last forever. However, it will cost an additional $50,000 each year to keep the security system maintained and up-to-date.

It is your decision whether to buy the security system or take your chances. Other than the information above, is there any other information you would like before making the decision? Explain your answer.

(continued)

Viruses --

4. Presume that you have all the information you need to make an informed decision about buying the security system. Would you buy it? Explain why or why not.

Because people rely on computers and the Internet to make a living, many firms offer computer security services for a fee. One way that a few of these firms generate business is by hacking into a company's computer system without permission. No damage is done nor is information stolen. The intent is to show how vulnerable a company's computers are to attacks by criminals. The belief is that if a security firm can prove there is a problem, a company will be willing to buy security services from that firm.

5. Do you think that hacking into a company's computer system by a security firm in order to get the company's attention should be legal or illegal? Explain your answer.

The Changing Concept of Privacy -------------------

THERE IS AN OLD STORY about a New Yorker on his first trip to Texas. The New Yorker was visiting a rancher in West Texas. Amazed that they could drive for more than half an hour and still be on the same ranch, the New Yorker asked the rancher how big his ranch was. The Texan politely refused to answer the question. What the New Yorker did not know was that asking a rancher about the size of his ranch is considered rude in Texas. It is like asking a person how much money that person makes.

In any society, there are certain facts and opinions that are considered personal and private. However, as society and its technology change, so does the concept of privacy. Today, we can use the Internet to find out how much money people make, how much they paid for their house, how old they are, and whether or not they have been convicted of a crime. Because this information is easily available, some people who may otherwise not be nosy might look up personal information about their friends and neighbors, simply because they can.

Record your answers below. Use another sheet of paper, if necessary.

1. List three pieces of information that people should not be able to find out about other people on the Internet. For each, explain why this information should not be available.

One of the ways that people use the Internet to find personal information about others is to *google* them. This neologism (new word) may appear in the dictionary someday. The process is simple; one visits www.google.com, and types someone's name (within quotation marks) in the search box. For some famous people, you will find that there are numerous references to them on the Web. For example, entering the name "George Bush" returns over 1.1 million web "hits."

Some people google their neighbors or friends. Many people google themselves to discover what information about them is out there on the web. Some adults google people with whom they are romantically interested.

(continued)

The Changing Concept of Privacy – – – – – – – – – – – – – – – –

2. Google yourself or an older adult in your home. If it is a common name, it may be hard to distinguish from other names. It may be helpful to add more identifying information. For example, enter your name (in quotation marks) and the name of your city in the search box. You might also add places of employment, the name of the school attended, and so forth. (If you need to, review the discussion in the book's introduction about Boolean searching.)

   • What, if anything, did you find?

   • Did finding this information (or not finding anything) surprise you? Explain why or why not.

   • Do you think that it is a good thing or a bad thing to find one's name on the Internet? Explain your answer.

3. List and describe three situations where you personally might want to google someone else.

4. Some people think that googling another person is sneaky and unethical. Do you agree? Explain why or why not.

(continued)

The Changing Concept of Privacy - - - - - - - - - - - - - - - -

5. Imagine that you are interested in a new romantic relationship with someone. How would you feel if you found out that they googled you before deciding whether or not to go out with you? Explain your answer.

   • Would you google the other person before deciding whether or not to go out with them? Explain why or why not.

6. Studies have shown that as people grow older, they tend to be more concerned about privacy issues than do younger people. Discuss this with an older adult or two. Then write why you think that people of different ages have different concerns about privacy.

Cyber Crime -----------------------------------

SOCIETY WILL ALWAYS have trouble with "technological lag." *Technological lag* is the fact that people can invent technology before we figure out how to control that technology. For example, nuclear power is the least expensive way to generate electricity. However, there are currently no nuclear power plants under construction in the United States. This is because, although we know how to generate electricity using nuclear power, we are not certain that we know how to safely deal with nuclear waste.

The Internet provides another example of technological lag. The Internet has proved itself to be of great benefit to society. However, society has not figured out how to prevent crimes from being committed using the Internet. Illegal downloading, discussed in Activities 5, 6, and 7 in Unit 4, is one of the biggest concerns for law enforcement and the entertainment industry today. Pornography, discussed in Activity 8 in Unit 2, is another major concern. These are only a few of the ways that the Internet is being used to commit crimes today.

Record your answers below. Use another sheet of paper, if necessary.

1. Do you think that someday society will be able to completely prevent all crimes from being carried out through the Internet? Explain why or why not.

2. One of the ways that people commit crimes through the Internet is by "stealing time." This may sound weird, but it is a big problem. Instead of spending money on huge computers themselves, some companies rent the use of other companies' computers. The rental fee is based on the amount of time a company uses another company's computers during a period. Some computer criminals illegally enter computers through the Internet, using the computers without paying rent. Years ago, American laws recognized the crime of larceny. Larceny involves stealing someone else's property. However, the crime of larceny required the property to be tangible. You may know that a tangible item is something that you can physically touch, like a table or a piece of fruit. Why did legislatures have to change the definition of larceny when computers were invented? Explain your answer.

(continued)

Cyber Crime -

3. Use of the Internet to commit fraud is another problem. A common example of Internet fraud occurs when someone tries to buy something using the Internet. A person may pay for something and then never receive the item they paid for. Even worse problems may occur when a criminal discovers a person's credit card number and makes unauthorized charges on that card. By its very nature, the Internet does not provide face-to-face sales transactions. Because the Internet has created so many new business opportunities, new businesses are created on-line everyday. This means that we are not always sure how reliable and trustworthy many web businesses actually are. Think about these issues, and then create three rules for safe Internet shopping. Be certain to explain each rule thoroughly.

_____'s Three Biggest Rules for Safe Internet Shopping

(your name)

1.

2.

3.

(continued)

Cyber Crime -

One reason that it is sometimes easy to commit fraud on the Internet is *channel effect.* Because many people view Internet as sophisticated and prestigious, they believe that claims made on the Internet must be true. This channel effect has caused significant problems for some of the elderly.

Some older people have health problems and need very expensive medicines. Some older people have not been able to find medications that adequately help them with their medical conditions. For these reasons, some older people look for miracle cures. Some web sites offer honest discounts on effective, proved medicines. However, other web sites are guilty of committing fraud against sick people. They do this by claiming their products can cure illnesses when it has not been proved that they can.

4. What would you tell an older person about using the Internet to find inexpensive medicine? Explain your answer.

Will the Internet Become a Necessity? - - - - - - - - - - - - - - -

YOU HAVE HEARD of automobile accidents involving drivers who were allegedly too old to drive safely. Of course, teenagers are not exactly famous for safe driving, either. The United States may have more problems with youthful and elderly drivers than many other countries. This is because many American communities arose or were greatly expanded after World War II ended in 1945. When the war ended, many returning soldiers and sailors married and started families. This created a huge demand for new housing. The housing demand contributed to the spread of American suburbs. The end of the war also affected the automobile industry. Demand for military equipment decreased after the war. Some of the automobile companies that had expanded their factories during the war focused on the civilian market after the war. People moved farther and farther away from inner cities beginning in the late 1940s, because cars made it possible to live relatively far away from where people worked, shopped, and went to school.

As a result, many members of American society considered an automobile an absolute necessity. Many teenagers today need access to a car in order to conduct everyday activities. This is also true of many elderly people.

Record your answers below. Use another sheet of paper, if necessary.

1. Do you believe that the Internet will become as much of a necessity for everyday life as the automobile? Explain why or why not.

2. Technological diffusion is the process of technology becoming available to everybody who wants it. For example, it is believed that almost everybody in the United States who wants to have a telephone now has one. The same is true of televisions. In what year do you believe that everybody in the United States who wants Internet access in his or her home will have it? Explain your answer.

(continued)

Will the Internet Become a Necessity? - - - - - - - - - - - -

3. Of course, the concept of technological diffusion notes that some people may never want a particular technological item. You may know somebody who does not want to own a television set. That person can usually provide several reasons why. Similarly, some people can afford to have a computer with Internet access in their home but have decided against it. List and describe three reasons why a person might decide against having Internet access at home.

4. Do you agree with any of these reasons? Explain why or why not.

5. Do you believe the reasons why people decide against owning a television are similar to, or different from, the reasons people decide against having Internet access at home? Explain your answer.

The objectives of this unit are to help students

- realize that different groups of people value the Internet in different ways
- recognize that the Internet can exacerbate inequities and disparities, as well as benefit society
- understand the need to balance the competing ideological, political, and social interests affected by the Internet
- develop an understanding of the Internet's ability to foster intentional communities

THE INTERNET may prove to be a mixed blessing. This unit is designed to help students evaluate the benefits as well as the challenges that the Internet presents to society. Students also weigh the impact that the Internet has on people of different backgrounds and viewpoints.

In this Unit. . .

El Internet: Latinos and the Internet provides students with demographic information about Latinos and their Internet habits. Students use this information to explore how this rapidly growing segment of the United States' population views the Internet.

The Age Gap asks students to explore the reasons why older Americans are less likely to embrace the Internet. Students engage in creative problem solving to make the Internet more senior-friendly.

Is the Internet Accessible to People with Disabilities? provides students with the opportunity to investigate how members of the disabled community perceive and use the Internet.

The Dumb Computer has students evaluate the relationship between information and power.

Voting on the Internet asks students to anticipate the consequences of allowing on-line political elections.

Criminal Registries provides students with the opportunity to assess the propriety of posting criminal records on-line. Students also investigate the appropriate scale and scope of on-line criminal registries.

How Is the Internet Changing Society? has students focus on the sociological and psychological impact of the Internet.

Cyberporn includes an exercise in which students create a Venn diagram to distinguish between constitutionally protected speech and unprotected speech.

Tensions in the Library asks students to evaluate the efforts of the federal government to regulate access to certain types of content on the Internet.

Cyber Crud engages students in the development of criteria for evaluating the reliability of information obtained on the Internet.

Can History Be Rewritten? has students scrutinize the use of the Internet as a means of

(continued)

documenting history and as a means of denying history. Students compare and contrast sites concerning the Holocaust as well as sites denying the Holocaust. Students are then asked to write an essay evaluating the possibility of using the Internet to successfully rewrite history. *Please note that students may be exposed to disturbing images and passages when conducting their research on the Internet.*

Hoaxes and Urban Legends allows students to examine the impact of Internet hoax phenomena and generate a list of tell-tale clues that commonly appear in hoax messages.

Hate Sites presents students with the task of balancing freedom of speech with society's need to protect its citizens. Students also investigate how they would respond if they were members of a group attacked on a hate site.

Cheatin' asks students to assess the impact of Internet-based affairs on romantic relationships. Students also evaluate the propriety of using software to catch a cheating partner.

On-line Doctors has students explore the growing trend in on-line medicine and examine the challenges people face when seeking access to medical care.

THE INTERNET MEANS different things to different people. For some of us, it is primarily for entertainment. For others, it is a tool used for work or school. For many people, the Internet serves both functions at different times.

The Internet is changing the way people communicate. In the process, it is also changing the way we look at our world. This is because distance, borders, and time no longer limit our ability to communicate with others the way they once did.

> "The Internet is changing the way people communicate."

The Internet is more than just communication technology. It is also information technology. It is often said that information is power. Many observers believe that the Internet is capable of shifting the economic and social power of different groups of people. The degree of this shift is still uncertain.

However, the Internet has already affected the lives of many people. People's expectations about what they should know and when they should know it are changing. The material that is available on the Internet has helped many people; some have been harmed. Laws have had to change to meet the challenges the Internet provides. In this unit, we will look at some of these developments, and try to better understand the Internet's role in society.

El Internet: Latinos and the Internet - - - - - - - - - - - - - - - - -

WHEN DISCUSSING LATINOS, we mean Americans of Hispanic and/or Latin American background. According to the U.S. Census Bureau, Latinos may be of any race. You may already know that Latinos are the fastest growing ethnic group in the United States. There are currently over 37 million Latinos in the United States. This is a little over thirteen percent of the total United States population. The Census Bureau estimates that Latinos will make up about twenty-five percent of the total United States population within the next fifty years.

In the United States, a 2002 Census Bureau study found that Latinos are more likely to live in the West and the South than in the Midwest and Northeast. The Census Bureau also found that Latinos are more likely to live in the center of large cities than non-Latino white people. In addition, the Census Bureau found that Latinos tend to be younger than non-Latino white people. Almost thirty-five percent of Latinos are under the age of eighteen, compared to less than twenty-three percent of the non-Latino white population.

1. One of the reasons that the Latino population in the United States is growing is because of immigration from other countries. Forty percent of Latinos in the United States today are foreign born. Why do you think people immigrate to one country from another? List and describe three reasons.

2. Why do you think the Latino population is younger than the non-Latino white population? Explain your answer.

3. Why do you think that Latino people are more likely to live in inner cities than the non-Latino white population? Explain your answer.

(continued)

El Internet: Latinos and the Internet - - - - - - - - - - - - - - - -

4. Why do you think that Latino people are more likely to live in the West and the South than in the Midwest and Northeast? Explain your answer.

Another study, conducted in 2003 by the UCLA Center for Communication Policy, found that a lower percentage of Latinos use the Internet compared to non-Latinos. Of Latinos under age thirty-five, seventy-one percent use the Internet, compared to ninety percent of non-Latinos in that age group. Of Latinos age thirty-five or older, less than half (forty-six percent) use the Internet, compared to almost two thirds (sixty-four percent) of non-Latinos in that age group.

In addition to different usage based on age, a gap was found in Internet use between Latino men and women. The UCLA study found that more than two thirds (sixty-eight percent) of Latino men use the Internet, compared to slightly more than one half (fifty-one percent) of Latino women.

5. Why do you think that Latinos age thirty-five or older are less likely to use the Internet than non-Latinos of the same age? Explain your answer.

6. Why do you think that Latino males are more likely to use the Internet than Latino females? Explain your answer.

(continued)

El Internet: Latinos and the Internet - - - - - - - - - - - - - - - -

Just as non-Latinos do, Latinos use the Internet as a source of both information and entertainment. However, Latinos are more likely to emphasize the use of the Internet for information than non-Latinos. In the UCLA study, seventy-five percent of Latinos said that the Internet is either a "very important" or an "extremely important" source of information for them. This compares to sixty percent of non-Latinos who said that.

7. Why do you think Latinos are more likely to emphasize the use of the Internet for information than non-Latinos? Explain your answer.

8. The UCLA study also investigated how reliable Latinos believed the information on the Internet was. Based on the information above, do you think that Latinos are more likely to trust the information they find on-line than non-Latinos are? Explain your answer.

The Age Gap --------------------------------

STUDIES INDICATE that over two thirds of all Americans use the Internet on at least an occasional basis. However, less than twenty percent of people over the age of sixty-five do so.

Record your answers below. Use another sheet of paper, if necessary.

1. List and describe three reasons why you think people over the age of sixty-five are less likely to use the Internet than other people.

2. List three features that people over the age of sixty-five would find especially useful on the Internet. Next to each thing you list, explain why you listed that item.

3. Look at some of the most visited web sites on the Internet, such as Yahoo (www.yahoo.com), MSN (www.msn.com), CNN (www.cnn.com), and eBay (www.ebay.com). After looking at these pages, list three things that you think make it difficult for people over the age of sixty-five to use those pages. Describe how you would fix each problem.

4. People talk about a *generation gap,* which means that members of an age group often have trouble understanding the beliefs, habits, and lifestyles of other age groups. Generation gaps operate in both directions—a younger generation of people has trouble understanding an older generation, and vice versa. Do you think the growing importance of the Internet in American society contributes to the generation gap or not? Explain your answer.

Is the Internet Accessible to People with Disabilities? - - -

HUMAN DISABILITIES can take many forms. They include mental disabilities, such as below normal intelligence, or an illness, such as schizophrenia. Disabilities also include physical differences, such as missing limbs or the inability to use a body part. Some of us have a disability. All of us know people with disabilities.

Many adaptive technologies have been designed to help people with disabilities use computers. Once computer use becomes possible, Internet usage also becomes possible. In fact, the computer offers some advantages to the disabled community over some other sources of information. For example, somebody who is unable to hold a book or newspaper may be able to use adaptive technology to find and read the same information on the Internet. For people who do not have full mobility because of a disability, the Internet may provide a means of better interacting with other people.

Record your answers below. Use another sheet of paper, if necessary.

1. Adaptive technology includes devices that allow people with impaired fine motor skills in their hands to use a computer without having to type on a regular keyboard. Another example of adaptive technology is software that speaks the words that appear on a web page for people who are blind. What would be another useful form of adaptive technology that would help people with disabilities use the Internet?

2. Suppose that you are a teenager with a disability. Adaptive technology is available to help you use the Internet. However, this technology can be very expensive. If your family could not afford this technology, should the government use taxpayers' money to provide you with adaptive technology? Explain why or why not.

3. One of the benefits of the Internet is that it allows users to form virtual communities. For example, a deaf person can meet other deaf users on-line to discuss some of the issues they face in society. Other than this and the benefits already listed above, list and describe another benefit that the Internet can offer to people with disabilities.

(continued)

Is the Internet Accessible to People with Disabilities? - - -

It is common for many types of businesses to aim their efforts at niches in the market. A *niche* is a small segment of the market for a product. For example, the Apple computer company emphasizes two niches. Its less expensive computers are aimed at students. Its more advanced computers are marketed to people who work in graphic arts. Another example: MTV is aimed at teenagers, VH1, owned by the same company, is aimed at older viewers.

4. Some niche markets consist of people with disabilities. Imagine that you are a person who uses a wheelchair. You have normal motor skills in your hands, so you do not need adaptive technology to use the Internet. Presume that you already own a satisfactory wheelchair. What other types of products specific to your disability would you try to buy through the Internet? List three and provide an explanation for each.

5. Section 508 of the Rehabilitation Act Amendments of 1998 requires all of the federal government's web sites to be usable by people with disabilities. Visit the White House's official web site: www.whitehouse.gov. Scroll down to the bottom of the front page of the site and click on "Accessibility." Read the Accessibility page. Then write one of the ways that the White House's web site attempts to make itself easier for use by people with disabilities.

   • What type of person with a disability would benefit from this? Explain why.

The Dumb Computer -

MANY PEOPLE CANNOT AFFORD to buy a computer, which with a monitor and printer can cost $1,000 or more. You may already know that much of the expense of a computer is not because of the hardware, but the software. Software allows the computer to operate (system software) and provides different uses for the computer (application software). For example, operating-system software like Windows XP or Mac OS 10, which is required to run most computers, can cost $100 to $200. A word-processing application program like WordPerfect costs about $45. A full "productivity suite" with word processing, database, and spreadsheet capabilities, such as Office XP, costs over $250.

If some people cannot afford a computer, that means that they will not have the same access to the Internet and other computer features that other people enjoy. Some people in the computer industry, and people concerned with the needs of poor people, have advocated for relatively inexpensive "dumb computers." A dumb computer is one that has very little software included on it. For example, a dumb computer may not have programs for word processing or creating spreadsheets. A dumb computer also would not have games or graphics packages. What the dumb computer provides is access to those types of programs by allowing Internet access to web sites where those programs are available. Thus, a fancier name for a dumb computer is an "application service provider."

Record your answers below. Use another sheet of paper, if necessary.

1. Some people talk about a "digital divide." The concern here is the gap between people who have easy access to computers and the Internet (the "haves") and those people who do not have easy access to computers and the Internet (the "have-nots"). Explain why you think the "digital divide" could pose problems for society.

(continued)

The Dumb Computer -

2. Imagine that you do not have easy access to the Internet, but all your classmates do have easy access. Describe what disadvantages you have because of your lack of access.

3. As mentioned in the Internet Buzz for this unit, "it is often said that information is power." Explain what this statement means.

4. How would the availability of relatively inexpensive "dumb" computers enable people with little money to have more power?

Voting on the Internet -

THERE ARE MANY DIFFERENT LAWS concerning voting in elections among the fifty states. There are also federal laws, some of which are in the United States Constitution, that concern voting. Originally, the federal government allowed only white men to vote. Some states later allowed black men to vote. In 1870, the Fifteenth Amendment of the United States Constitution gave black men the right to vote throughout the country (although some states still tried to prevent this). A few states allowed women to vote beginning in the late 1800s. In 1920, the Nineteenth Amendment of the United States Constitution gave women the right to vote throughout the country. In 1964, the Twenty-fourth Amendment of the United States Constitution prohibited poll taxes. Poll taxes required that people pay for the right to vote, which kept many poor people from voting.

Record your answers below. Use another sheet of paper, if necessary.

1. Today, many states are considering laws to allow people to vote in political elections on the Internet. Some people believe that it should not be too easy to vote. These people are against allowing people to vote on the Internet. Explain why you think some people are opposed to Internet voting.

Because American men as young as eighteen could be drafted and sent to fight in Vietnam during the 1960s, many Americans argued that the voting age, which was twenty-one at the time, should be lowered to allow eighteen year olds to participate in the election of politicians. The Twenty-sixth Amendment, passed in 1971, lowered the voting age to eighteen. However, since 1971, it has been found that teenagers who have the right to vote rarely do so. In fact, there seems to be a correlation between age and voting participation—the older an American is the more likely he or she is to vote. Nevertheless, it has been found that fewer and fewer people have been voting in the United States since 1960.

2. Why do you think that so many young people do not vote?

(continued)

Voting on the Internet --------------------------

3. Why do you think that so many older people do vote?

4. If people were allowed to vote on the Internet in all elections, do you think more young people would vote? Explain why or why not.

5. Who do you think is more likely to vote today—a rich person or a poor person? Explain your answer.

6. If people were allowed to vote on the Internet in all elections in the future, do you think more rich people would vote than do today? Explain why or why not.

7. If people were allowed to vote on the Internet in all elections in the future, do you think more poor people would vote than do today? Explain why or why not.

Criminal Registries -

IN 1994, MEGAN KANKA, a seven-year-old girl from New Jersey, was raped and killed by a neighbor who had twice before been convicted of sex offenses. Megan's parents called for legislation that requires the government to disclose information about convicted sex offenders living in a community. New Jersey quickly adopted "Megan's Law," and a federal version of the law took effect in 1996. Every state now has laws that require certain types of criminal offenders to register with law enforcement agencies. These registries contain information such as the name, address, criminal record, and photograph of those registered. The most common type of criminal registry is for sex offenders.

In more than a third of the states, these registries are now available on-line. This means that any Internet user can find the current address of some convicted criminals, as well as other information. In March 2003, the United States Supreme Court ruled that the posting of convicted sex offenders' photographs and addresses on the Internet was constitutional. However, the court's decision was not unanimous; several members of the court disagreed. They said that being made to register was a form of punishment, and that this was unfair because some people had to register many years after they had committed, and been punished for, the crime in question.

The definition of a *sex offender* includes those who have committed sexually oriented crimes against children and adults. Understandably, many people are concerned about these types of offenders living or working in their neighborhood. Many parents have praised Megan's Law and laws like it as helpful in keeping their children safe.

Record your answers below. Use another sheet of paper, if necessary.

1. Do you believe that information about convicted sex offenders should be posted on the Internet? Why or why not?

2. Regardless of how you answered question 1, presume that information about sex offenders living in your state is available on the Internet. Should anyone who uses the Internet be able to access information about sexual offenders, or should access be limited? Explain your answer.

(continued)

Criminal Registries----------------------------------

3. Members of the United States Supreme Court disagree on whether or not being made to register as a sex offender is a form of punishment. Do you believe that requiring people to register as sex offenders is punishment? Explain why or why not.

4. Some registered sex offenders have been harassed by other people who found information about those offenders on the Internet. Do you think that people who harass those offenders should be punished? Why or why not?

In some states, sex offender registries include types of sex crimes such as prostitution. Some people are opposed to the requirement that people convicted of prostitution must register. These people say most of those who engage in prostitution do so because they are drug addicts. Some people say that prostitution can be considered a "victimless" crime when it is between two consenting adults. Some argue that if there are victims of prostitution, they are the prostitutes, who have allowed drugs to take control of their lives and force them into degrading activities.

5. Do you think that information about people convicted of no crime other than prostitution should be available on the Internet? Explain why or why not.

6. Although the first wave of on-line criminal registries focused on sex crimes, people have argued for an expansion of criminal registries. Some people believe that all criminal records, regardless of the type of crime or how long ago the crimes occurred, should be available to the public. Do you agree with allowing Internet availability for all criminal records? Explain why or why not.

7. If you believe that all criminal records should be available on-line, do you also believe that anybody should be able to view those records? Or would you limit access to certain types of people or organizations? Explain your answer.

How Is the Internet Changing Society? - - - - - - - - - - - - - - - -

FIVE HUNDRED YEARS AGO, before widespread literacy (the average person could not afford books) and electrification, people had relatively few reasons to stay at home, other than to eat, sleep, or do household chores. Things changed as technology changed. Advances in printing technology made printed materials, such as books and newspapers, more accessible to people. Electrification brought the radio and television (and electric lights to read by) to our homes. Sociologists (people who study how groups behave) and psychologists (people who study how individuals behave) are concerned about how these technological changes have changed the way that people interact with each other.

The Internet has also brought significant change to human interaction. Today, it is possible to do all of the following things using the Internet: shop for food, clothing, and shelter; pay bills and do banking; communicate with friends and coworkers; work at home; do research for schoolwork; and take classes. This has economic consequences. For example, shopping-mall owners have found that people are spending less time per visit at malls. There are also social consequences. Some sociologists and psychologists have discussed the fact that many Americans are less likely to join clubs and other organizations than they were in times past.

Record your answers below. Use another sheet of paper, if necessary.

1. Why do you think many sociologists and psychologists are worried about the Internet? Explain your answer.

2. The Internet does not *make* people stay at home; it *allows* people to stay at home. Why do you think people are deciding to stay at home more? Explain your answer.

(continued)

How Is the Internet Changing Society?---------------

Virtual communities are places on the Web in which people can meet without physically meeting. These virtual communities include chat rooms, e-mail, blogs, and other developing electronic communities. Some observers are concerned that the Internet will cause problems for society in two different ways. Some people with Internet access may spend less time actually in the physical presence of other people. Those who may not have Internet access—the poor or elderly—may suffer other types of social problems.

3. Why would spending less time in the physical presence of other people cause problems for a person? Explain your answer.

4. Why would having no access to the Internet create social problems for people? Explain your answer.

Cyberporn -

THE FIRST AMENDMENT of the United States protects freedom of speech. Speech includes the words and images a person posts on the Internet. However, freedom of speech is not absolute. Certain types of speech, including threats and words that encourage violence, are not protected by the First Amendment. This means that a person who threatens to hurt another person can be convicted of a crime.

Another type of speech that is not protected by the First Amendment is obscenity. People who post words or images on a web page that is found obscene can be convicted of a crime. In the 1972 case *Miller v. California,* the Supreme Court provided us with a list of tests to determine whether a message is obscene:

- The message will be judged using the standards (viewpoint) of the local community where the criminal trial is being conducted.

- The message will be judged according to the viewpoint of the average person in that local community.

Presume that a government prosecutor files charges of obscenity against a person responsible for a web site (webmaster). Using the standard of an average person in the local community, trial jurors would be asked to look at the contents of a web page. Then, they must decide all of the following:

- The web page appeals to a prurient interest (*prurient* is defined on the next page).

- The web page is obviously offensive.

- The web page lacks any serious literary, artistic, political, or scientific value.

Note that there is a difference between pornography and obscenity, at least in the eyes of the law. *Pornography* is any material that is considered sexual or erotic in nature. The First Amendment protects some pornography. If a court decides that a pornographic item is obscene, the First Amendment does not protect that item.

(continued)

Activity 8 *(continued)*

Cyberporn--

A Venn diagram is a graphic representation of a relationship between two or more things or ideas. For example, many types of birds can fly. However, not all birds can fly. Some animals, such as bats, can fly but are not birds. So

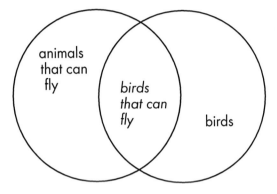

1. Draw a Venn diagram that displays the relationship between pornography, obscenity, and Internet pornography. (**Hint:** Your diagram will have three circles.)

2. *Prurient* means that something appeals to a shameful interest in sex. Are all discussions of sexual topics shameful? Explain why or why not.

Before the Internet, people interested in pornography could find it in "adult" bookstores or at "adult" movie theaters. Pornography could also be found in some movie rental stores, usually separated from the rest of the store's videos. In these situations, the only people who were exposed to pornography were those who were seeking it. With the growing number of Americans gaining access to the Internet in their homes, there is the increasing possibility that many people will see pornography even if they do not want to.

(continued)

Cyberporn -

Of course, adults are able to use parental controls to shield their children from some pornography, as discussed in Activity 2 in Unit 4. However, few observers believe that the problem of accidental exposure to Internet pornography can be eliminated.

3. What do you believe is the best way to protect Internet users from viewing pornography that they do not want to see? Explain your answer.

4. Trial jurors are people chosen at random from the community in which they live. If summoned for jury duty, it is a crime to refuse to serve on a jury unless one has a very good reason. These reasons include being the mother of a preschool child, or being too ill to serve. As discussed on page 44, if a webmaster is prosecuted for obscenity, jurors must look at the allegedly obscene web site. Do you believe that people who do not want to be exposed to allegedly obscene material should be excused from serving as a juror at that trial? Explain why or why not.

Tensions in the Library- -

MANY LOCAL LIBRARIES and schools receive money from the federal government. This money is used to help libraries and schools maintain the resources the public expects and needs. Today, one of the resources the public expects and needs is Internet access. In 2000, the federal government enacted a law known as the Children's Internet Protection Act (CIPA). CIPA requires schools and libraries that receive federal funds to prevent minors from gaining access to certain web sites. CIPA describes minors as people under the age of seventeen. The web sites that must be blocked include those that have obscene material, and other web sites with material that is "harmful to minors." The American Library Association challenged the new law, but the United States Supreme Court ruled CIPA constitutional in 2003. This means that schools and libraries that receive federal funds must follow the requirements in CIPA to use a "technology protection measure," such as software that is similar to parental controls. (For more on parental controls, see Activity 2 in Unit 4.)

The United States government's annual budget is over $2 trillion ($2,000,000,000,000—or 2 million *times* 1 million dollars). Other levels of government, including cities and states, are eligible to receive money from the federal government. The federal government makes this money available to local governments for projects that the federal government wants the local government to administer. For example, federal highway funds are given to states to build and repair highways. Federal funds are given to many colleges and universities to help students pay for school. Federal funds are also given to cities and towns to help equip police departments. In addition, federal funds are given to help libraries provide Internet access.

When the federal government provides money to state and local agencies, it typically mandates (requires) that those agencies spend the money in certain ways and not spend it in other ways. For example, highway funds must be spent on highways, not day-care programs. Day-care funds must be spent on day-care programs, not highways. However, it becomes more complicated than that. For example, when the federal government wanted the states to lower the speed limit on highways to 55 m.p.h. in the 1970s, it threatened to take away highway funds from states that failed to lower the speed limit.

Answer the following questions. Use another sheet of paper, if necessary.

1. It has been said, "the one who controls the purse strings controls public policy." Explain what this saying means.

   • Do you agree with this saying? Explain why or why not.

(continued)

Tensions in the Library- -

2. One group of critics of the Children's Internet Protection Act said that the law is "one of the more massive giveaways to a private industry in recent memory." Which industry will profit from CIPA regulations? Explain your answer.

Leaders in San Francisco estimated that the city's libraries receive around $20,000 a year from the federal government. However, officials there decided not to use filtering software, risking the loss of that money.

3. Suppose you live in San Francisco. Like other residents of that city, you pay state, local, and federal taxes. Some of those taxes go to support the city's public libraries. As a taxpayer, how would you have reacted to the officials' decision that risked losing federal funds for the libraries?

4. Again, suppose you live in San Francisco. Like other residents of that city, you use its public libraries. As a *library user*, consider your reaction to the decision to risk losing federal funds for the libraries. Would that reaction have been the same as your reaction as a *taxpayer*? Explain why or why not.

Some people are concerned that blocking Internet access from some sites may hurt teenagers. For example, since Internet filtering programs block access to sites where certain words about sex and the human body appear, teenagers may not be able to access web sites that talk about health issues, such as sexually transmitted diseases.

5. Which is more important to you—protecting young people from Internet pornography, or allowing young people to use the Internet to find information about sexually transmitted diseases? Explain your answer.

The Internet and Society

Cyber Crud -

WHEN PEOPLE are conducting research for school, work, or their personal lives, they often use a school or public library. The books, publications, and other materials in schools and public libraries have been "mediated." This means that if a library item claims to be reliable and truthful about its subject, somebody or a group of people has verified that the information is trustworthy. Information on the Internet is not mediated. Much of the information on the Internet is informative and truthful. However, for very little expense, anybody can create a web site and post information that is misleading, incomplete, or dishonest.

Record your answers below. Use another sheet of paper, if necessary.

1. Does the Internet pose a threat to information gathering—does it make spreading "misinformation" easier? Or does the Internet help us learn the truth? Explain your answer.

2. Sometimes "facts" can be merely what a group of people decides they are. (For example, who decides what a dollar is really worth?) If enough people decide to believe that something is true, does that make it true? Explain why or why not.

3. There are certain basic rules for evaluating the quality of information from any source, including web sites. Write some of the criteria for determining whether or not a web site's information is reliable. The list is started for you below.

   • Who is the author of the information? What do we know about him or her? What can we find out about him or her?

   • What are the sources of the web site's information? Can the reliability of those sources be determined?

   • Is the information written in a nonbiased manner? Or is it written in a manner that is trying to persuade the web site's visitor to adopt a point of view?

(continued)

Cyber Crud --

Your additions to this list:

-

-

-

4. Should there be a government agency in charge of supervising the Internet to maintain the reliability of information? Explain why or why not.

5. Many people believe that a **URL** (web address) that ends in .org belongs to a not-for-profit association. Is this true? Do some Internet research on the topic. Start at a search engine like Google or Excite. Write the address of each web site you visit until you find an answer with which you are satisfied.

What did you find—are all .org's not-for-profit associations, or not?

Can History Be Rewritten?----------------------------

THE HOLOCAUST—the mass execution of Jews and other persecuted groups by the Nazis during World War II—occurred during the early to mid 1940s. For various reasons, including bigotry against Jewish people, there are those who deny that the Holocaust actually occurred. With the passage of time, most of the survivors and other witnesses of the Holocaust have died or are quite old. Because of this, many people are concerned about the ability of a few people to make others doubt that something as horrible as the Holocaust really occurred.

Visit each of the web sites below. The first group of web sites discusses the importance of the Holocaust as an historical event. The second group of web sites denies that the Holocaust occurred. These two groups of web sites are in conflict with each other. The first group presents what is accepted as historical fact, while the other side argues for a rewriting of that history.

Historical View of the Holocaust:

motlc.wiesenthal.com/resources/education/revision/
www2.ca.nizkor.org/index.html
www.holocaust-history.org

Revisionist View of the Holocaust:

www.ihr.org
www.air-photo.com
www.revisionisthistory.org

After reviewing these web sites, decide whether historical facts can be revised. Then write an essay that supports that view. Remember, the argument is not whether the Holocaust occurred—no serious scholar doubts that. The question that should be answered in your essay is whether or not a small group of people might someday be able to use the Internet to successfully rewrite history. You will need to use another sheet of paper.

Hoaxes and Urban Legends -

INTERNET HOAXES are e-mail messages that are usually untrue. Hoaxes are usually written with the intent that the e-mail message will be forwarded to as many people as possible. Some hoaxes prey on your sense of fear. These include computer virus hoaxes ("If you get a message that says 'happy birthday' don't open it . . ."). There are also hoaxes about the potential for personal harm ("Don't go to the mall this Saturday because . . ."). Some hoaxes prey on people's sympathy for others who are sick or in trouble ("Little Jane Doe is suffering from leukemia and wants to receive as many e-mails as she can . . .").

Because of the ability of the Internet to transmit graphics, some Internet hoaxes take the form of photographs. These photographs have been edited to create pictures of events that did not really happen. (For example, there are fake pictures on the Internet, allegedly taken from a satellite, that show the explosion of the Columbia shuttle in February 2003.)

A common form of Internet hoax is the urban legend. Urban legends existed many years before the invention of the Internet. They are stories about something bad that supposedly happened to someone else that could happen to you if you are not careful ("Watch out for hidden hypodermic needles that are attached to . . .").

Record your answers below. Use another sheet of paper, if necessary.

1. Most hoaxes can be spotted by the intelligent observer. List below three words or phrases that are likely to appear in the title or body of an Internet hoax. Explain why each word or phrase is probably a tip-off that the message is a hoax.

2. Why do you think people create Internet hoaxes? Explain your answer.

(continued)

Hoaxes and Urban Legends -

3. Do you think people who create Internet hoaxes should be punished? Explain why or why not.

4. Some people say that the Internet makes us smarter because it puts so much information at our fingertips. Other people say that the Internet makes us dumber because there is so much *misinformation* at our fingertips. Which view do you agree with? Explain why.

5. People in business and in government are concerned that Internet hoaxes actually end up costing money. This is true even when an Internet hoax does not ask anybody to send money to someone. Explain how Internet hoaxes can cost society money.

Hate Sites -

A HATE SITE is an Internet site operated by individuals or groups who promote hatred or hostility toward others based on their religion, race, ethnicity, sexual orientation, or other characteristics. The United States Constitution's First Amendment protects freedom of speech. The First Amendment protects most hate sites. Of course, First Amendment protection is not complete protection. (As former Supreme Court Justice Oliver Wendell Holmes once said, the First Amendment does not allow someone to falsely yell "fire!" in a crowded movie theater.)

First Amendment scholars have pointed out that the First Amendment is not used to protect popular speech. Popular opinion protects popular speech. First Amendment protection becomes an issue when someone's message is generally unpopular. Most hate speech is unpopular.

The ease with which a person can communicate on the Internet has taken hate speech to new levels. Any person who is bigoted against a group of people can easily set up a web site that targets that group for abuse. Clearly, when the First Amendment was adopted in 1791, the Internet was not a consideration. However, neither were television and radio.

Record your answers below. Use another sheet of paper, if necessary.

1. Under what circumstances, if any, should hate speech on the Internet be made illegal? Explain your answer.

Imagine you are one of a group of people whose skin is purple. An anti-purple people web site, www.ihatepurplepeople.org, is created. The web site says that all purple people are stupid, commit crimes, and smell bad. The web site says that all purple people should leave the United States and "go back where they came from."

2. What do you think would be the best way(s) for you and other purple people to respond to this web site? Evaluate each of the following choices. Provide your reasoning for each.

   • Do nothing—just ignore the hate site.

   • Send e-mails to the webmasters of the hate site, asking them to stop putting anti-purple people messages on the Internet.

(continued)

Hate Sites -

- Send e-mails to the webmasters of the hate site, threatening them with lawsuits and other legal action unless they stop.

- Have somebody try to "hack" into the web site and get rid of it.

- Create a pro-purple people web site that tells the truth about purple people—that other than the color of their skin, they are just like everybody else. This web site would not mention www.ihatepurplepeople.org.

- Create a pro-purple people web site that discusses each of the claims made at www.ihatepurplepeople.org and points out the errors in each claim.

- Create a pro-purple people web site that is aimed mostly at criticizing www.ihatepurplepeople.org and the people who run that web site.

3. Which of the choices in question 2 do you think is the best? Explain your answer. If you think there is an even better choice that is not listed above, describe it here.

Cheatin' -

MANY PEOPLE are now using the Internet to look for a romantic partner—a boyfriend, girlfriend, husband, or wife. Unfortunately, some of these people are already involved in a relationship. Some people who are already in a romantic relationship become involved in what are called "on-line affairs."

Record your answers below. Use another sheet of paper, if necessary.

1. Many of those who become involved in on-line affairs claim that this is not really cheating, as long as they never meet the other person(s) face-to-face. Do you agree? Explain why or why not.

2. Suppose that you are involved in a relationship. You discover that your partner is involved in an on-line affair. Your partner (truthfully) tells you that he or she has never met the other person face-to-face. Describe what your reaction would be.

There are now several software programs available to try to catch partners in on-line affairs. These programs, called "spyware," allow people to secretly check on their partners' computer usage. This is legal as long as the spyware is installed on one's own computer. For example, if a husband and wife share a home computer, the wife can legally install spyware on that computer without having to tell her husband.

3. Suppose that you are involved in a relationship. You and your partner share a computer. You are not involved in an on-line affair. In fact, you have no interest in such an affair. However, you discover that your partner has secretly installed spyware on the computer. Describe what your reaction would be. What, if anything, would you say to your partner?

On-line Doctors

A 2003 STUDY by the Pew Internet and American Life Project (www.pewInternet.org/reports/pdfs/PIP_Health_Report_July_2003.pdf) found that 80 million adult Internet users, or approximately 93 million Americans, have used the Internet to look up medical information. The study found that one of the reasons that people look up medical information on the Internet is that the information is available twenty-four hours a day. Many of us feel ill late at night or on the weekends, when it is difficult or impossible to see a doctor or other medical provider.

Three quarters of those surveyed said they believed the Internet improved the health information and services they received. Of course, for many people, it is uncertain whether this is a fact or a perception.

Record your answers below. Use another sheet of paper, if necessary.

1. List three ways to tell whether a health information site is providing reliable information. Explain each item.

Many people live far away from a doctor's office. The Internet has helped create a new group of so-called "distance doctors" who practice "telemedicine." Some Americans live hundreds of miles from a hospital. In some rural school districts, school nurses are now able to consult on-line with doctors about sick students. The nurse can record some of the student's vital signs, such as temperature and blood pressure. The nurse then relays this information to the doctor, who is able to see and talk to a sick student on camera.

In some less developed countries around the world access to health care has, until now, been unavailable. Technology is now allowing doctors and other health care providers to perform certain parts of a medical exam over the Internet. Because the Internet is not restricted by international boundaries, neither is telemedicine. A doctor in Chicago or any other city can consult with a patient in any country in the world.

One problem with this new technology is who should pay for it. Many people who live in poor rural areas, whether in the United States or other countries, simply cannot afford medical care.

(continued)

On-line Doctors ------------------------------------

Nor can they afford to pay for the Internet technology that allows medical care to be brought to them. In the United States, some of the financial burden is assumed by government programs that are paid for by American taxpayers. The governments of some other countries are not able to afford these programs.

2. Medical technology and Internet technology continue to improve rapidly. Do you think that someday the average patient will not have to visit a doctor's office to receive adequate medical care? Explain why or why not.

3. Who should pay for the medical care for poor people? Does it make a difference in which country a poor person lives? Explain your answer.

You are probably not surprised that medical school is very expensive for students. Some programs provide scholarships for medical students who promise to practice medicine in areas of the United States where there currently are not enough doctors.

4. Why do you think that some areas of the United States do not have enough doctors? Explain your answer.

5. Many medical schools receive money from taxpayers in the form of government support for medical studies. Do you think your tax dollars should be used to encourage doctors to work in areas where there are currently not enough doctors?

6. As discussed in Activity 7 in Unit 1, many college students around the world can now earn college degrees on-line. Distance education technology is currently being used to provide refresher courses for doctors. These doctors have already attended traditional medical schools. Do you think that someday a medical student will be able to get an adequate education through a 100 percent on-line medical school? Explain why or why not.

The objectives of this unit are to help students

- understand the commercial nature of the Internet
- recognize the pervasiveness of commercialism and advertising in American culture
- understand how demographic and psychographic differences operate in American society
- rely on their own creativity and imagination in generating strategies for the relatively new medium of the Internet
- develop their knowledge of financial and economic matters
- use problem-solving skills in a variety of contexts

THE INTERNET began as a noncommercial medium but was soon embraced by the marketplace. Teenagers are attractive to producers of consumer goods and services; these firms are aggressively exploiting teenagers' fascination with the Internet. One of the primary purposes of this unit is to help students become better informed and more discerning consumers.

You are likely familiar with the growing body of research that demonstrates the importance of helping students identify career choices beginning at approximately the age of twelve. The second major purpose of this unit is to expand students' awareness about career opportunities in Internet-related businesses as well as other areas of commerce.

In this Unit. . .

Portals: Where Do You Start? offers students the chance to develop and design a web portal that would be attractive and interesting to teenagers.

The Demographics of Doritos provides information about the snack food maker's efforts to use the Internet to capture the attention of teenagers, and asks students to evaluate the efficacy of those efforts.

The Psychographics of Sprite has students focus on how businesses use the interactivity of the Internet to study teenagers' values and attitudes.

Privacy Policies has students investigate how the Internet helps businesses gather personal data about Internet users.

Spam focuses on recent efforts to combat unsolicited e-mail and asks students to appraise both the merits of spam and proposed regulations dealing with spam.

Deregulation introduces students to a recent decision by the Federal Communications Commission that allows increased concentration of ownership of media outlets. Students assess the need for diversity of viewpoints in society and the role of the Internet in promoting diversity.

(continued)

The World Wide Web's Life Cycle provides information about the product life cycle and asks students to anticipate the future of some types of Internet businesses.

The Domain Name Game offers a case study that requires students to identify relevant facts. This activity also provides the opportunity for students to use their creativity as they generate new names for web sites.

What Happens to the Mom-and-Pop Store? provides students with the opportunity to explore the economic impact the Internet has on small businesses.

Is Anybody Clicking? asks students to appraise Internet advertisers' efforts to generate consumer response and has students identify successful advertising practices.

The Internet and the Job Market focuses on the Internet's ability to shift jobs, and requires students to analyze the ethics of substituting prisoners and overseas workers for current United States wage earners.

Credit Cards and the Internet has students assess the Internet's effect on consumer debt.

Whither AOL? calls for creative problem solving. AOL needs to change its delivery method in order to survive; students decide what AOL should do. Students also interpret a graph to ascertain stock market prices and to assess their willingness or aversion to undertaking financial risks.

THERE ARE MANY ways to make money by doing business on the Internet. A **portal** is a site where many people begin their visit on the Internet. Some of the best-known portals include MSN and Yahoo. Portals offer specialized content, such as local weather, television and movie listings, sports scores, and local news. This content gathers an audience for the companies that advertise on those portals.

> **"On-line marketplaces bring a group of different sellers and buyers together."**

Another way of making money on the Internet is to provide content that people will pay for. For example, web sites for newspapers and magazines sell articles to people who want to buy them. Music sites allow visitors to download music for a fee. Some content providers allow free downloads and make money by selling advertising at their sites.

Virtual storefronts use the Internet to sell products directly to individuals or businesses. Perhaps the best-known example is Amazon.com, which has no traditional stores and sells its products only through the Web. Other companies use a "bricks and clicks" approach. For example, Target and Wal-Mart have actual store buildings that shoppers can visit, and both retailers also sell products on the Internet.

On-line marketplaces bring a group of different sellers and buyers together. These sites include eBay and Priceline.com. These sites make money by charging a commission for their service. This commission is usually a percentage of the price of the items sold on the site.

These are only some of the existing Internet business models. Undoubtedly, new methods of making money on the Internet will arise in the future. This unit examines some of the most common forms of Internet-related businesses. We will also examine how the Internet is affecting non-Internet businesses. In addition, we will explore the impact the Internet may have on your own career.

Portals: Where Do You Start? -

MANY INTERNET USERS have established start pages or home pages where they begin their World Wide Web surfing. Examples include My Yahoo, My Excite, and My MSN. These sites are attractive because they allow users to collect information that is important or interesting, such as local news and weather, television listings for favorite channels, information about favorite entertainers and sports teams, or a daily horoscope. These sites are also called portals, because they are the "door" through which a surfer enters the World Wide Web.

In this exercise, you will design a portal that will be attractive to teenagers. Probably the best way to start is to look at the popular portals listed above—My Yahoo, My Excite, and My MSN. If you use an Internet Service Provider (**ISP**) like AOL or EarthLink, it probably offers a portal site.

1. In the space below, show what categories of information will be available to users. It is probably best to allow users to customize the information they can access within each category. For example, users in different cities may only want to know about the weather in their hometown. Different users will also have different tastes in music, movies, and so forth.

Try to design a portal that is at least as good as the portals currently available. But be creative— try to design a portal that is better than any existing portal. And remember, you want to design a portal that will be interesting to teenagers. A good portal allows users to customize not only information; it also allows users to customize the appearance of the page.

(continued)

Portals: Where Do You Start? - - - - - - - - - - - - - - - - - -

2. For each category or object available on your portal site, explain below why you want to offer that category or object.

Category/Object	Explanation

3. Explain why your portal would be more attractive to teenagers than currently existing portals.

4. Most portals earn money for their owners by selling advertising space on their portal sites. List three advertisers that you think would want to advertise on your portal site, and explain why.

The Demographics of Doritos -----------------------

PEPSICO, the maker of Pepsi, also owns Frito-Lay, the company that makes Doritos. For several years, Doritos were heavily advertised during the Super Bowl. The Super Bowl attracts a huge television audience, so advertisements broadcast during the game are very expensive. In 2002, Doritos dropped its traditional Super Bowl advertising campaign and tripled its Internet advertising budget instead.

Demographics are statistics about people grouped by such information as age, gender, ethnicity, geography, and income. Businesses, such as Frito-Lay, study demographics to determine the **target market** for their product. Doritos' target market is twelve- to twenty-four-year-olds, and is more likely to be male than female.

According to Jonathan Glicksberg, director of client services at Atmosphere, Doritos' Internet advertising agency, "The teen target has a lot of skepticism toward marketing activities on-line, but if we align with the content they're interested in—entertainment, music, games—it allows us to engage with them in a more meaningful way."

1. Visit the Doritos web site (www.doritos.com). List and describe three ways that the Doritos web site tries to attract and keep your interest.

2. What information about you does the Doritos site try to get?

3. Why do you think the company that makes Doritos wants this information?

4. Describe how you think the company that makes Doritos uses this information.

(continued)

The Demographics of Doritos -

Doritos spends much more money on Internet advertising than most other companies that make food products—about nine percent of its total annual advertising budget, as compared to an industry average of about one to two percent.

5. Do you think the people who handle Doritos's advertising made the right decision when they decided to discontinue their Super Bowl advertisements and spend the money on Internet advertising instead? Explain why or why not.

Cammie Dunaway, who was in charge of marketing Frito-Lay's products to children and teens, said, "We want to make sure teens are talking about and thinking about Doritos all the time, and it is impossible to do that without having a significant presence on-line."

6. Do you agree or disagree with Dunaway? Explain why or why not.

The Psychographics of Sprite -

OF COURSE, Doritos is hardly the only product on the Internet that is aimed at teenagers. Advertising on the Internet takes two basic forms: advertising banners and web sites maintained by an advertiser. For example, suppose you are reading a news story at a portal, such as MSN.com. The MSN site may have a banner advertisement for Abercrombie and Fitch—even though you were not looking for information about clothing, you have now seen the advertisement. Often, a banner advertisement is a **click-through.** This means that if you click on the banner advertisement you will be led to Abercrombie and Fitch's own web site (www.abercrombie.com). A company can track the number of click-throughs that different banner advertisements generate. This is the value of **interactivity** to the company—it now knows what types of advertisements work and what types to avoid.

Abercrombie and Fitch's web site is publicized in the company's magazine advertisements and in promotional displays in its stores. The web site allows you to shop on-line. It also includes music downloads, photographs of models, e-mail postcards that you can send to friends, and other items. These features are also interactive. For example, if many visitors to the site click on one type of postcard, but not another, the company learns what types of pictures are popular with its consumers and what types of pictures are not.

Sprite's web site (www.sprite.com) allows visitors to play video games, listen to and remix music, and enter contests. If someone believes that he or she can have fun at the Sprite web site, he or she will visit the site. While at the site, a visitor is exposed to several advertisements for Sprite and other products. Visitors can get information about new products and find out about their favorite NBA star or musical group. Sprite carefully studies what is and is not popular with visitors based on which activities visitors take part in or avoid. For example, if a feature on a certain hip-hop artist at the Sprite web site gets a lot of hits, Sprite knows that the artist is still popular with Sprite drinkers. Sprite will continue to feature that artist at its web site and in other advertisements. If another artist gets only a few hits, Sprite knows that it needs to search for other, more popular artists to include in its advertising.

The owners of Abercrombie and Fitch and Coca-Cola, the owner of Sprite, know who their target demographic group is—teenagers. Both companies also study the **psychographics** of their target market. Psychographics are statistics about people grouped by their interests, attitudes, values, and habits (including buying habits). Most teenagers would not let older adults choose their music or clothes for them. In order to get you to buy their products, the adults at Abercrombie and Fitch need to find out what you are into, as does Sprite. The interactivity of the Internet helps them do this.

(continued)

The Psychographics of Sprite -------------------

Record your answers below. Use another sheet of paper, if necessary.

1. Visit the Abercrombie and Fitch web site and the Sprite web site. You are a teenager. Abercrombie and Fitch wants your attention, as does Sprite. After visiting their web sites, do you think these companies did a good job or not? Explain why or why not.

2. Do the owners of the Abercrombie and Fitch web site seem to understand what people your age are interested in now? Or is the site out of date? Explain your answer.

3. Pina Scarra, the director of youth brands for Sprite, said that Sprite wants teenagers to think, "You know, Sprite understands me. Sprite is . . . one of us." After looking at the Sprite web site, do you think Scarra has done a good job? Explain why or why not.

4. Interactivity allows Internet users to tell the owners of web sites how they feel about things. This may be especially important to teenagers, who are learning about independence and becoming their own person. Do you feel that the interactivity of web sites like Sprite's and Abercrombie and Fitch's gives you more power? Explain why or why not.

5. Surveys tell us that Abercrombie and Fitch is currently the store most often named by American teenagers as their favorite clothing store. Abercrombie and Fitch does not advertise on television. Do you think that Abercrombie and Fitch's decision not to advertise on television while maintaining an interactive Internet site has helped the company gain favor among teenagers? Explain why or why not.

Privacy Policies -

THE FEDERAL TRADE COMMISSION (FTC), a government agency, has created (and enforces) laws dealing with various privacy issues. For example, the FTC protects privacy regarding health care—your doctor, pharmacist, and insurance company need to know your medical history, but your neighbor should not. The FTC also works to protect financial information, such as bank records.

In 1998, the FTC enacted the Children's Online Privacy Protection Rule, under the direction of Congress. This rule applies to operators of commercial web sites and on-line services directed to children under the age of thirteen, and to general audience web sites and on-line services that knowingly collect personal information from children under thirteen. Among other things, the rule requires that web sites get consent from a parent or guardian before the web sites can collect personal information from children.

What happens when someone turns thirteen? Does she or he still have privacy rights when surfing the Web? The short answer is yes, but in truth, it is not that simple. Commercial web sites must have a privacy policy. There is usually a link to these privacy policies on the bottom of a web site's front page. However, it has been found that few people actually check a web site's privacy policy. In addition, the requirement for a privacy policy is only that there must be a privacy policy—this policy does *not* have to be one that actually protects you! A web site's privacy policy can actually be that the site makes no effort to truly protect a visitor's privacy, if the visitor is at least thirteen years old.

Many web sites also place a **cookie** on your computer. That cookie identifies you to the web site when you return to it, or to other web sites that share cookies with one another.

Answer the following questions. Use another sheet of paper, if necessary.

Click on one of the web sites that you visit the most. Look at the bottom of its front (or start) page for a link to its privacy policy. Click on the link, and read the privacy policy.

1. Do you understand everything that the privacy policy tells you?

   • Explain your answer, giving three examples from the privacy policy (these examples can be things you do understand or that you do not understand).

(continued)

Privacy Policies ----------------------------------

2. After reviewing this privacy policy, do you feel comfortable that the owner of the web site is protecting your privacy? Explain why or why not.

3. With whom, if anybody, does the owner of the web site share information about you?

   • Are you comfortable with this sharing? Explain why or why not.

4. Why do you think the web site owner wants personal information about you? Explain your answer.

5. What does the privacy policy tell you about the web site's use of cookies?

   • Do you understand how the web site uses cookies? Explain why or why not.

6. Do you think the average adult is aware how, or if, his or her privacy is protected when that person surfs the Internet? Explain why or why not.

Spam -

YOU PROBABLY already know that *spam* is bulk unsolicited e-mail. *Bulk* means that the e-mail was sent to many (perhaps millions) of people at one time. *Unsolicited* means that the recipients of the e-mail did not ask to receive e-mail from the sender. For example, if Juan visits a travel web site and asks to be placed on a subscription list for low cost airfares, e-mails from the travel web site about low cost airfares are not spam. This is because Juan asked to receive those e-mails. However, if Patti receives e-mail from a company she has never heard of before offering to sell her something, that is spam because Patti did not ask for the e-mail.

Many companies rent their mailing lists. These include people's addresses for United States mail and e-mail. For example, if you subscribe to a magazine, chances are that the magazine is paid by other companies to send mailings to you. Similarly, if you register your e-mail address at a web site, the owner of that web site may receive money from other companies to send you unsolicited e-mails.

Many people are aggravated by spam, and have asked Congress to pass laws to control it. However, there are differences of opinion about what types of activities should be prohibited or required by anti-spam legislation. One proposal is called an *opt out* plan, which means that if someone receives an unsolicited e-mail, that person should be able to ask the sender to take him or her off the list of recipients of future e-mail from that sender.

Currently, many spammers' e-mails seem to offer a chance to opt out. However, some spammers are dishonest about the "opt out" choice. Instead, they fraudulently offer the "opt out" choice to see if people will respond. Suppose Wesley gets an unsolicited e-mail that offers a chance to opt out by clicking on an "unsubscribe" link. When Wesley clicks on the link, he is telling the sender that his e-mail address is active. Some dishonest spammers will then see this as encouragement to continue sending spam to Wesley. Presumably, any new law that requires spammers to give e-mail users the chance to unsubscribe will require spammers to actually take those people off their subscription lists.

Some members of the public are asking Congress to pass antispamming laws that require e-mail users to "opt in" before receiving e-mails. This would include the situation above in which Juan asked the travel web site to alert him about low cost airfares. However, many legitimate companies rely on unsolicited e-mails to sell their products and services. They argue that the only way they can expand their business is to be able to solicit business from people who may need their product or service but do not yet know about the company sending the e-mail. These compa-nies argue that an "opt in" requirement would hurt or even ruin them. Unsolicited e-mail is not only sent by for-profit businesses. Many not-for-profit groups, including charitable organizations, send unsolicited e-mails to help raise money for charitable and other social needs.

(continued)

Spam -

Record your answers below. Use another sheet of paper, if necessary.

1. Describe the difference between an "opt out" requirement for spam and an "opt in."

2. Which requirement do you think is a better idea for consumers? Explain your answer.

3. Describe a major advantage to the public that results from unsolicited e-mails.

4. Describe a major disadvantage to the public that results from unsolicited e-mails.

5. Most people have received "junk mail," or unsolicited advertisements, through the United States mail ("snail mail") for years. Why do you think that many people are more upset about spam than they are about junk mail that is more traditional?

Deregulation -

THE FEDERAL GOVERNMENT has the constitutional power to regulate interstate and foreign commerce. This means that the federal government can make rules regarding businesses that operate across state and national boundaries. Because radio and television broadcasting are interstate businesses, the Federal Communications Commission (FCC) regulates them. In order to operate an AM or FM radio station or a broadcast television station, the owner of that station must first obtain a license from the FCC.

Because the amount of airwave frequency space for broadcast radio and television is limited, the FCC has rules on how many radio and television stations one company or person can own. The FCC has these rules on ownership in order to make sure that the public is served by a diverse group of media outlets. Diversity, it is hoped, will provide different points of view to the public. The FCC does not control the Internet. This is due in part to the fact that space on the Internet is not limited in the way that radio and television broadcast space is limited.

In June 2003, the FCC changed its rules on media ownership. It decided that media companies could own more television and radio stations than was previously allowed. There are five commissioners on the FCC, and the decision by the FCC to change the rules was not unanimous. Three commissioners said that they were not worried about the diversity of viewpoints available in the media. They said

> Today we can access news, information, and entertainment in many enhanced and non-traditional ways via: cable and satellite television, digital transmission, personal and portable recording and playback devices, hand-held wireless devices, and perhaps the most extraordinary communications development, the Internet. In short, the number of outlets for national and local news, information, and entertainment is large and growing. . . . The Internet, as an entirely new medium . . . completely transformed the way in which we communicate in unimaginable ways. . . . Whereas other forms of media allow for only a finite number of voices and editorially-controlled viewpoints, the Internet provides the forum for an unlimited number of voices, independently administered.

Two commissioners objected to the new rules. Commissioner Michael Copps said that he disagreed with the decision to change the ownership rules,

> because today the FCC empowers America's new Media Elite with unacceptable levels of influence over the media on which our society and our democracy so heavily depend. . . . I see centralization, not localism; I see uniformity, not diversity; I see monopoly and oligopoly, not competition. . . . What about the vaunted 500-channel universe of cable TV saving us? Well,

(continued)

Deregulation -

90 percent of the top cable channels are owned by the same giants that own the TV networks and the cable systems. More channels are great. But when they're all owned by the same people, cable doesn't protect localism, editorial diversity, or competition. And those who believe the Internet alone will save us from this fate should realize that the dominating Internet news sources are controlled by the same media giants who control radio, TV, newspapers, and cable."

Commissioner Jonathan S. Adelstein said, "This is a sad day for me, and I think for the country. . . . In the end, [the change in ownership rules] simply makes it easier for existing media giants to gobble up more outlets and fortify their already massive market power."

Record your answers below. Use another sheet of paper, if necessary.

1. Explain what a *diversity of viewpoints* means.

2. Do you think this diversity is important in the media? Explain why or why not.

3. Do you agree with the three commissioners who decided to change the media ownership rules? Or do you agree with the two commissioners who did not want this rule change? Explain your answer.

4. Do you think that the Internet has added to the diversity of viewpoints in today's society? Why or why not?

The World Wide Web's Life Cycle - - - - - - - - - - - - - - - - - - -

THINK ABOUT how our news and information sources are paid for. Daily newspapers usually cost less than $1, which is barely the cost of the newsprint that they are printed on. Newspaper publishers rely on advertising revenue (money paid to newspapers by advertisers) to make a profit. Similarly, the price we pay for most magazines does not result in a profit for the magazine publisher. As with newspapers, advertising revenue is the real source of magazine publishers' profit. Broadcast television and radio are free to consumers, because broadcasters earn their profit from the companies that advertise on their stations. Consumers must pay for cable television access, but then, many of us have access to over fifty channels on our cable systems.

Many commercial (for profit) World Wide Web sites make money for their owners in one or both of two ways. One is to sell advertising on the web site. For example, when you visit Yahoo or MSN, you will probably see several advertisements at those web sites. Some web sites also make money for their owners by selling content. Examples of this include the web sites for newspapers, such as the *New York Times* (www.nytimes.com). If a visitor wants to download an article that appeared more than a month ago in the *Times,* the visitor must pay for the convenience. Another example of a web site that sells content for a fee is BuyMusic (www. buymusic.com), which sells music files that can be downloaded.

People in the business of selling goods or services are aware that most products have a life cycle.

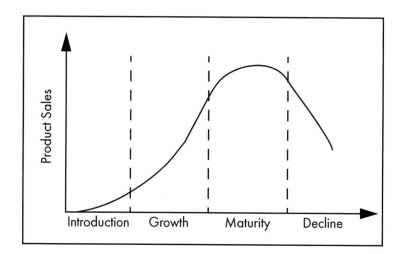

When a product is new, the product life cycle is in its introductory stage. There are two different pricing strategies for a product in the introductory stage. One pricing strategy is called *penetration pricing,* which attempts to price a new product as low as possible in order to get

(continued)

The World Wide Web's Life Cycle - - - - - - - - - - - - - - - - -

as many people to try the product. Once people are in the habit of using a product, the price can be raised to a more profitable level. An example of the use of penetration pricing occurred in the banking industry. Automatic Teller Machines (ATMs) cost banks many millions of dollars. However, for several years after the introduction of ATMs, most bank customers could use ATMs for only a few cents per transaction or perhaps no charge at all. Once many banking customers got into the habit of using ATMs, banks began to increase the price for using ATMs.

Another pricing strategy for new products is called *skimming,* which is the opposite of penetration pricing. Sometimes a product's manufacturer wants to attract those consumers known as "innovators" or "pioneers." This group of people is often willing to pay extra for the chance to use a new product before other people do. For example, when the Chrysler PT Cruiser was introduced in 2000, Chrysler dealers found that they could charge a higher than average price. This was because some people were willing to pay extra to be the first to have a PT Cruiser in their neighborhood. As the PT Cruiser became more common, the price dropped to a normal level as other people began to buy the vehicle.

Record your answers below. Use another sheet of paper, if necessary.

1. Consider the product life cycle of web sites on the World Wide Web. Do you think most web sites are still in their introductory stage of the life cycle? Or do you think they are now older than that? Explain your answer.

2. If you were going to develop a new commercial web site that sold content for a fee, which introductory pricing strategy would you use—penetration pricing or skimming? Explain your answer.

(continued)

The World Wide Web's Life Cycle - - - - - - - - - - - - - - - - - -

3. Most of us gain access to the World Wide Web through an Internet Service Provider (ISP). Examples of popular ISPs include AOL, MSN, and Earthlink. A subscription to an ISP costs between $10 and $100 a month, depending on the level of service. ISPs must compete with each other for customers. Do you think the cost of access to the Internet will increase, decrease, or stay the same over the next three years? Explain your answer.

4. You may already know that the largest retailer on the Internet is Amazon.com. Amazon has yet to consistently make a profit since it began operating in 1995. (Amazon lost nearly $150 million in 2002.) However, many investors are still excited about Amazon, and are willing to invest their money in Amazon. Why do you think these investors are so optimistic about Amazon?

The Domain Name Game -

A WEB SITE'S ADDRESS is technically called its *URL,* or *uniform resource locator.* The web site's address is also known as a domain name, such as www.walch.com. Today, Internet commerce is becoming increasingly important. Thus, one consideration when creating a new company name is to make sure that nobody is already using that name on the Internet. Some companies have also bought domain names that could be used by others to criticize their company. For example, PJX Corporation might buy the domain name www.ihatepjx.com to prevent somebody else from using that name on the Web.

The Nissan Motor Company was founded in Japan in 1933. The company has been selling cars in the United States for more than forty years. It originally called its car line Datsun. In 1982, the company decided to change the name of its car line to Nissan. In 1991, a man named Uzi Nissan formed a company called Nissan Computer Corporation. In 1994, Mr. Nissan created the web site www.nissan.com. He used the web site to sell computers and computer services. Nissan Motor Company was upset and asked Mr. Nissan to stop using the web site. Mr. Nissan refused to do so. In 1999, Nissan Motor Company filed a lawsuit against Mr. Nissan.

Record your answers below. Use another sheet of paper, if necessary.

1. Which of the facts above support Mr. Nissan's argument that he should be able to continue to use www.nissan.com? Explain why.

2. Which of the facts above support Nissan's Motor Company's argument that Mr. Nissan should not be able to continue to use www.nissan.com? Explain why.

3. Who do you think should win the lawsuit? Explain why.

4. Search on the web and find out what happened in the lawsuit between Nissan Motor Company and Uzi Nissan. Write your findings here.

(continued)

The Domain Name Game -

5. A federal law passed in 1999 forbids "cybersquatting." Cybersquatting occurs when somebody registers a domain name that intentionally uses the trademark of somebody else. The cybersquatter then demands a high price to sell the name to the company who owns the trademark. Do you think Mr. Nissan was guilty of cybersquatting? Explain why or why not.

According to NetFactual (www.netfactual.com) the most common letters for the start of a web site's name (after the usual "www") are S, C, M, and T. The least common letters are X, Q, Z, Y, J, and K. This makes sense, when you consider the frequency of these as beginning letters in English words. (You can check this by comparing the number of pages devoted to words that start with the letter S in a dictionary, and the number of pages devoted to words that start with X.)

Businesses want to stand out from other businesses. Distinctive names can help. For example, when Standard Oil of New Jersey wanted a new name it decided on Exxon. Exxon is distinctive because only one language in the world (Maltese) uses a double x. Kodak is another distinctive example of a made-up company name. Words that begin with the letter K are uncommon, and words that begin and end with the letter K, even more so.

6. Suppose that you and your friends want to start a new company. The company will make clothes that will be popular with teenagers. First, you need to create a name for this company. You know that the name should not already be used by somebody else; the new name should be distinctive and attention getting; and the name and its web address should be easy to remember. What are you going to name your company? Explain why.

What Happens to the Mom-and-Pop Store? - - - - - - - - - - -

IN THE LATE nineteenth century, big businesses began to mass-market goods to the American public. Technology made this possible. The new railroads reached from coast to coast. This allowed goods to be shipped anywhere in the United States. Advances in printing technology made magazines and newspapers cheaper, allowing more people to read them. Companies bought space in these magazines and newspapers to advertise their products. New printing technology also made it easier and cheaper to print catalogs. This led to the rise of large mail-order companies. Many local manufacturers and local merchants went out of business because they could not compete with the big new national companies.

In the late twentieth century, the Internet arose. Large Internet merchants, such as Amazon.com, have forced many small local bookstores to close. The ability for travelers to use the Internet to buy airline tickets and make hotel reservations has caused many travel agencies to go out of business. Stores that sell prerecorded music on CDs are also closing. Numerous other businesses have either failed, or will fail in the future, because of their inability to compete with the Internet.

Activity 8 in Unit 1 investigates the consequences to employees who lose their jobs due to technological unemployment. Here, we will look at the consequences to consumers.

Record your answers below. Use another sheet of paper, if necessary.

1. Three types of businesses that are threatened by the Internet are discussed above. List three other types of businesses that you think are threatened by the Internet. Explain why.

2. Mike Dreese, owner of Newbury Comics, the largest music retailer in the Northeast, has said that in the near future, "all involved with prerecorded music will suffer failure" because of the Internet. If you owned a store that made most of its money by selling CDs, how would you respond to the Internet's taking your business away? Explain your answer.

(continued)

What Happens to the Mom-and-Pop Store? - - - - - - - - -

3. One criticism about large companies is that they take away local choices and regional specialties, replacing them with uniform national products. Do you think that the Internet provides you with more choices of products and services than traditional companies, or fewer? Explain your answer.

4. Certainly, people who lose their jobs because of the Internet consider the Internet a bad thing. Do you, as a consumer, think that the Internet is a bad thing? Explain why or why not.

Is Anybody Clicking?- -

ONE WAY that companies make money from the Internet is by selling advertising space on their web pages. The most common Internet advertisement is the banner ad—a rectangular box that appears on a web page. Advertisers have two primary concerns when deciding whether to buy advertising space on a particular web site. One concern is determining how many people are visiting a web site on a regular basis. In addition, the demographics of a web site must be attractive to an advertiser. A teenager who visits a web site is probably not interested in buying real estate. An adult might be.

Web sites that sell advertising track how many people visit that web site each day, and many web sites have thousands, even millions, of viewers daily. However, it is one thing to see an advertisement, and another thing to buy what the advertiser is selling. While it is hard for an advertiser to know if an advertisement in a magazine is helping to sell its products, an advertiser can usually tell whether or not an advertisement on a web site is doing its job. This is because most advertisements on the Internet are *click-throughs*. In a click-through advertisement, the viewer is asked to click on the advertisement for more information, or to make an on-line purchase of the product being advertised. So far, and the Internet is still a relatively new advertising medium, click-throughs do not seem to work very well. Less than one percent of click-through advertisements are actually clicked on.

This is a problem for the companies selling advertising on the Internet. Advertisers can quickly find out whether or not their advertisements are helping them make money. This is because they can measure how many viewers actually clicked on their advertisements. As a result, many advertisers who were excited about the Internet only a few years ago and were willing to spend millions of dollars on Internet advertising have since decided to spend much less. Some companies have quit advertising on the Internet altogether. Some of the companies that hoped to make lots of money selling Internet advertising went from being "dot coms" to "dot bombs," and have gone out of business.

Record your answers below. Use another sheet of paper, if necessary.

1. Have you ever clicked on a banner advertisement? Explain why or why not.

Surf around the Web, looking at the different types of advertising that are currently being used on the Internet. Check out some of your favorite web sites. Make certain that you also visit such portals as MSN.com, Excite, Yahoo, and CNN. (If you hit the refresh button in your browser's toolbar, you might discover that the web site runs several different advertisements in the same location.)

(continued)

Is Anybody Clicking? -

2. Describe an advertisement you viewed that you believe is particularly good. Explain why you think this is an effective advertisement.

3. Describe an advertisement you viewed that you believe is particularly bad. Explain why you think this is not an effective advertisement.

Imagine that you are working for an advertising firm that designs Internet advertisements for companies that want to use the Internet to sell products.

4. List three things you would do to encourage Internet surfers to click on your advertisements. Next to each item, explain why you think it would work well.

5. Who do you think is more likely to click on an advertisement: a person surfing the Web for a school or work project, or a person surfing the web for pleasure? Explain your answer.

The Internet and the Job Market- - - - - - - - - - - - - - - - - -

THE INTERNET is transnational. This means that it does not stop at the borders of any country. As a result, many Internet businesses are also transnational. Because we are able to interact through the Internet around the world, Internet workers can be located anywhere. For example, if a web site for an American company offers customer service by e-mail, the customer service representative does not have to live in the United States. He or she might very well be in a part of the world where customer service representatives can be hired for a salary that is much lower than that of American workers.

Record your answers below. Use another sheet of paper, if necessary.

1. Some people in the United States are afraid that the Internet may cost some Americans their jobs. Other people say that the Internet creates more American jobs than it takes away. With which of these two viewpoints do you agree? Explain your answer.

2. Imagine that you are an American businessperson. Suppose that the average hourly wage for an American customer service representative is $10 an hour. The average hourly wage for an English-speaking customer service representative who lives in the mythical Notmycountry is $2.25 an hour. Would you establish your customer service office in the United States, or would you establish your customer service office in Notmycountry? Explain your answer.

Part of the rehabilitation process for prisoners is helping them learn job skills. (Chances are that prison inmates make the automobile license plates in your state.) Another source of inmate employment is the Internet. Internet customer service workers with whom you communicate may be inmates who are in prison.

3. Do you think that prison inmates should be able to work as customer service representatives on the Internet? Explain why or why not.

4. Do you think that prison inmates who are already working as customer service representatives should be paid the same wage as workers who are not in prison? Explain why or why not.

Credit Cards and the Internet -

COMPANIES THAT issue credit cards make money in several different ways. Some credit card companies charge customers an annual fee to use their card. Most credit card companies charge interest on outstanding balances. For example, Sara charged $500 on her credit card in May. When she receives the bill in June, she pays only $20, the minimum amount required by that credit card company. The company will then charge interest on the remaining balance. If the interest rate is twelve percent a year, or one percent a month, Sara now owes the credit card company $484.80:

$500 charged in May (−$20 paid in June) (+1% of $480) = $484.80.

Most credit card issuers charge compound interest. This means that credit card companies charge interest on interest. That sounds weird, but let us see what it means. We will again use Sara's situation.

$500 charged in May (−$20 paid in June) (+1% of $480) = $484.80 owed by Sara at the end of June.

What will Sara owe at the end of July if she does not use the card during that month? The answer:

$484.80 owed at the end of June (+1% of $484.80) = $489.65 owed at the end of July. Even though Sara did not use the card during the month of July, she now owes more money on the card than she did a month earlier.

Charging interest is not a crime. It is legal because we are borrowing someone else's money when we charge purchases on credit. The bank or other company whose money we are using is allowed to make a profit for lending us their money. Most credit card issuers today charge an annual interest rate of between 8 and 24 percent a year. However, "usury" is against the law. *Usury* is defined as charging an interest rate higher than the law allows.

Record your answers below. Use another sheet of paper, if necessary.

1. Usury limits vary from state to state. In fact, some states, such as South Dakota and New Hampshire, have no usury limits for credit cards. These states believe that credit card companies will only charge "what the market will bear." Explain what you think this statement means.

   • Do you agree with this statement or not? Explain your answer.

(continued)

Credit Cards and the Internet -------------------

2. The Internet does not stop at the state line. Suppose that you live in Massachusetts, which has usury limits. You are looking for a new credit card on-line, and you find one that looks good: You will be able to have your own customized design on the card, and the credit card issuer does not charge an annual fee. However, the credit card issuer is based in South Dakota, which has no usury limits. Which laws do you believe should apply regarding that credit card's interest rates—Massachusetts or South Dakota? Explain your answer.

Note that Sara in our example on page 84 did not pay off her entire credit card balance at the end of the month. This is quite common. The amount of credit card debt per American household has steadily increased the past few years, from an estimated $7,800 in 2000 to nearly $9,000 in 2002. Interest payments alone cost the average American household over $1,000 a year.

3. Why do you think Americans are charging more on their credit cards (and paying off less credit card debt) than they were a few years ago?

4. Do you think that the Internet is contributing to the increasing amount of credit card debt in the United States? Explain why or why not.

5. Most major credit card issuers, including MasterCard, Visa, Discover, and American Express, have policies that protect consumers against Internet fraud. Most credit card issuers provide 100% consumer protection in cases of Internet fraud. This means that when Internet fraud does occur, the credit card company often must bear the loss itself. Why do you think that credit card companies are willing to do this?

Review some of the Internet fraud protection polices of some major credit card companies:	
Visa	www.usa.visa.com/personal/secure_with_visa/zero_liability.html
MasterCard	www.mastercard.com/general/zero_liability.html
Discover	www.discovercard.com/discover/data/account/securityprivacy/shopping.shtml
American Express	www10.americanexpress.com/sif/cda/page/0,1641,5962,00.asp? CCNR=OZ4

Whither AOL? -

AOL (America On-line, Inc.) was until recently viewed as nearly synonymous with the Internet. In 2001, AOL controlled more than forty percent of the United States' household Internet Service Provider (ISP) market (over 26 million households). AOL has been relying primarily on dial-up service using ordinary telephone lines instead of higher-speed media, such as cable modem, DSL (Digital Subscriber Line), or satellite. Because of its reliance on dial-up service, AOL has begun to lose customers.

Dial-up service as a percentage of ISP service is expected to steadily decrease over the coming years. This is because more and more people are switching from dial-up connections to faster connections. Recent studies have shown that about a third of American homes now have high-speed connections. Telephone or cable television companies typically offer these faster connections. Wiring a community with telephone or cable lines is a huge investment. AOL has the same owner as the Time Warner cable television system, but does not own Comcast, Cox, Adelphia, or any of the other major cable television systems. We will presume that AOL is not able to buy any of these other cable television systems.

Record your answers below. Use another sheet of paper, if necessary.

Given this brief background, AOL is now investigating its options in cable modem, DSL, and satellite delivery methods.

1. Imagine that you are an executive at AOL. List three things you would do to make AOL more competitive with high-speed Internet providers. For each item, provide an explanation about why you think it would help the company.

_____'s Plan to Save AOL
            (your name)

1.

2.

3.

(continued)

Whither AOL? -----------------------------------

Since the merger of AOL with Time Warner in January 2001, the company's stock price has declined from nearly $60 a share to less than $20 a share in August 2003.

2. The chart above graphs the approximate price of Time Warner's stock from August 27, 2001, to August 26, 2003.

   • What was the highest price (approximately) for the stock during this period?

   • What was the lowest price (approximately) for the stock during this period?

One of the basic rules of thumb in the stock market is "buy low, sell high." This means that to make a profit in the stock market, a person should sell a share of stock for more than they paid for it. This has not been easy to do with Time Warner stock over the past few years.

3. People who buy Time Warner stock today believe that the price will eventually go up. Do you agree? Explain why or why not.

(continued)

Whither AOL? -

Another rule of thumb in the stock market is that the return on an investment should be based on its risk. For example, a United States savings bond is a very low-risk investment. Because of this, it pays the bondholder a low interest rate. Buying stock in the stock market is a much riskier investment. The price of a company's stock may soar upward and make some of its stockholders very wealthy. Alternatively, the price of that company's stock may go down to nothing, and possibly bankrupt some of its stockholders.

4. Presume that you will have enough money to be able to invest some of it someday. Do you think that you would be more likely to buy government bonds or to buy company stock? Explain your answer.

The objectives of this unit are to help students

- examine their Internet habits
- use the Internet to make significant decisions in their lives
- create their own web site
- investigate some of the ethical challenges that the Internet presents
- explore the interactivity of the Internet
- practice safe Internet usage

MANY TEENAGERS ARE already "power users" of the Internet. Thus, it is important that they develop a self-awareness of their Internet practices. This unit seeks to help students become discerning and effective Internet users. Several activities offer students opportunities to use the Internet to research important issues in their lives.

Because the Internet is designed to be easily accessed and facilitates rapid, widespread communication, it allows students' voices to be heard. However, the Internet can also be easily misused. This unit strives to assist students in adopting ethical standards for Internet usage.

In this Unit. . .

Blogs has students explore this medium of self-expression, and asks students to identify the purposes web logs serve for both the creators and their audiences. Students are invited to create their own blogs.

Parental Controls requires students to develop a series of guidelines for Internet access by young children. This activity can be completed individually or as a group activity.

Safe Chat is designed to be a group project. This activity asks students to generate a list of guidelines for young people using Internet chat rooms.

Defamation challenges students to assess some of the legal and ethical consequences of criticizing others on the Internet.

Downloading, Part I requires students to confront the ethical issues and practical consequences surrounding the illegal copying of music and movies.

Downloading, Part II provides a role simulation for students, who must act as a corporate executive in dealing with illegal downloading by employees.

Downloading, Part III encourages students to use their creativity to design an anti-downloading poster.

Buying a Car has students use the Internet to conduct the research necessary for the intelligent and informed purchase of a "big ticket" item.

Choosing a College, Choosing a Career provides students with the opportunity to systematically investigate their future opportunities.

For Whom Do I Vote? engages students in an on-line exercise to learn about the positions of candidates for political office.

The FBI's Carnivore introduces students to the FBI's e-mail searching system. Students then develop guidelines for balancing individual rights and national security interests.

YOU ARE THE FIRST generation of Internet users. In the future, when the history of the Internet is told, people will read how you and your friends began to develop patterns of Internet usage that may endure for

> **"Clearly, the Internet gives you power."**

hundreds of years. Or maybe not; perhaps some new technology will come along and make the Internet of tomorrow seem about as important as the telegraph of today. In the meantime, the Internet is proving itself a source of information and entertainment.

This unit asks you to view the Internet as a consumer. Yet it also provides you with opportunities to look at the Internet as a potential web designer or content creator. You may never own your own radio station or newspaper. However, you are able to design and launch your own web site. You can also use e-mail and newsgroups to tell people how you feel about something. Clearly, the Internet gives you power. With this power comes responsibility.

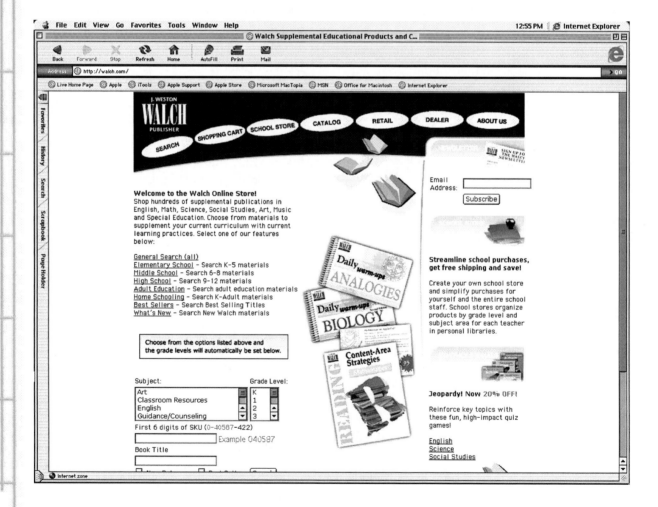

Blogs ---

"BLOG" IS COMMON SLANG for a web log. Web logs are Internet users' personal web pages. They often contain collections of the blogger's observations and thoughts, a record of the blogger's personal or professional activities, and links to other sites. Blogs are typically in chronological order, like a diary or journal. The most recent posting to the site usually appears on the top of the page.

Some people estimate that there are over half a million blogs today, read by millions of people. Many colleges host blog sites for their students, and some companies host sites for their employees. Some blogs are shared by a group of people who use the blog as a public place to discuss subjects in which they have a common interest, such as hobbies, careers, or favorite musicians and actors. Most blogs, however, are highly individualized. As blogger Cirilia Rose says, "While some blogs successfully supplement more traditional forms of news and commentary, the majority remains largely personal and narrow in scope and appeal."

Record your answers below. Use another sheet of paper, if necessary.

1. Some observers have pointed out that blogs allow individuals who are not rich or famous to be heard. Do you think that it is getting easier or harder for the average person to be heard in the world?

2. What role, if any, does the Internet play in a person being heard today?

3. Some people have compared blogs to bumper stickers on cars. Why do you think people put bumper stickers on their cars?

(continued)

Blogs -

4. Do you think that people create blogs for some of the same reasons they put bumper stickers on their car? Explain why or why not.

5. Suppose that a rich or powerful person told a big lie to the public. Do you think that an ordinary individual who knew the truth (and could prove it) would be able to use a blog or some other web site to get the public to understand the truth? Explain why or why not.

6. Why do you think people read other people's blogs? Explain your answer.

Anybody can create a blog. If you are interested in creating a blog of your own, you can visit blog hosting sites, such as new.blogger.com, www.diaryland.com, or www.blog-city.com. (These are only a few of the many free blogging sites available.)

Parental Controls -

BECAUSE YOU PROBABLY share a home with at least one older adult, you may have had at least one discussion about what is and is not appropriate for teenagers to view on the Internet. Clearly, many parents are concerned. Many parents subscribe to parental controls through their Internet Service Provider (ISP). AOL's television advertisements frequently discuss parental controls, as do advertisements for MSN. Other resources are also available, such as CYBERsitter, Net Nanny, and CyberPatrol. Besides parents, many educators use blocking services to keep certain sites from being viewed in schools.

Some of the most common types of information to be blocked from the view of younger users include sex, illegal activity (including illegal drug use), and sites that promote hate or intolerance of others. In addition, information about religious cults, tattoos, and gambling can also be blocked.

Record your answers below. Use another sheet of paper, if necessary.

1. How do you personally feel about parental controls that would prevent you from visiting certain web sites? Explain your answer.

2. Regardless of whether your school blocks or prohibits access to some web sites, imagine that your school has no such limitations. Any web site that anybody wants to visit would be available. Do you think this open access would cause problems in your school? Explain why or why not.

3. Imagine that you have an eight-year-old brother or sister. He or she is a frequent user of the Internet.
   - Would you want the computer that the eight-year-old uses to have parental blocking? Explain why or why not.

(continued)

Parental Controls ------------------------------------

- If you believe that an eight-year-old should be prevented from visiting certain types of web sites, list at least two types. Explain your reasoning for each.

4. Someday, you may be a parent or stepparent. What sorts of rules, if any, would you set for surfing the Internet for each of the following age groups? Explain each answer.

   - Four- to eight-year-olds

   - Eight- to twelve-year-olds

   - Thirteen- to seventeen-year-olds

5. If you become a parent or stepparent someday, do you think that you will have parental controls installed on your home computer? Explain why or why not.

6. Many colleges do not block access to web sites on the computers to which students have access. (One reason for this policy is that college students are usually eighteen or older.) However, many colleges prohibit students from creating a "hostile environment" while using a computer in any school area where others can see what is on the computer's monitor. How would you describe a hostile environment?

Safe Chat -- -- -- -- -- -- -- -- -- -- -- -- -- -- -- -- -- --

YOU HAVE PROBABLY already heard about bad things that happen because of Internet chat sites—weird stories like those about teenagers who think they are talking to a teenaged girl who turns out to be a middle-aged man, and so forth. One of the problems is that not all chat rooms have a moderator. A moderator is the person responsible for making sure that people in a chat room play by the rules.

You have probably heard or read warnings from older adults about possible problems in chat rooms. However, these warnings are probably more effective when they come from teenagers instead of older adults. Moreover, despite the warnings that many students may have heard about possible dangers in Internet chat rooms, the Internet Safety Education Foundation has found that approximately forty percent of the students it polled do not recognize the dangers of chatting on-line with strangers.

In groups, design a list of ten rules (they can be both "do's" and "don'ts") for young people who visit Internet chat rooms. Next to each rule, provide a brief explanation of why you think that rule should be on the list.

Safe Internet Chat Rules, According to _____

(your names)

1.

2.

3.

4.

5.

6.

7.

8.

9.

10.

Defamation -

YOU MAY ALREADY be familiar with the term "flaming," which occurs when someone criticizes someone else on the Internet. Usually, we think of flaming as being direct criticism, such as in an e-mail, instant message, or a chat room. However, it is not uncommon to see a web site criticize an individual or group of people to a large Internet audience. Of course, the First Amendment protects our right to speak freely, even if our belief or viewpoint criticizes others.

Sometimes, somebody tells a lie about another person that hurts that person's reputation. The person whose reputation has been damaged can sue for "defamation." The United States Supreme Court has told us that the First Amendment does not protect defamation. Defamation is not a crime in the United States, but if a person can prove their reputation was hurt by defamation, they can sue the other person for money.

Four things must be proved in a lawsuit for defamation:

- the statement made was not true *and*
- the person who made the statement knew, or should have known, that the statement was not true *and*
- the untrue statement damaged somebody's reputation *and*
- the person whose reputation was hurt can prove that the injury is worth money

Record your answers below. Use another sheet of paper, if necessary.

1. Suppose Jimmy lies and tells all his friends that Sheila is a thief. Sheila's boss hears this and fires Sheila. Sheila is out of work for a month before she finds a new job. Sheila may then hire an attorney and sue Jimmy for defamation.

    - How much money should Sheila be able to sue Jimmy for? Explain your answer.

(continued)

Defamation ---

2. Suppose that Andrea's blog says that a famous movie star "is a really mean person who hates a lot of his fans." Many people read Andrea's blog. Some of these people put links to Andrea's blog on their own web sites, or otherwise tell other people what Andrea's blog says. As a result, Andrea's comments are seen or heard by thousands of people in only a few weeks. Suppose that the movie star found out about Andrea's web site and now wants to sue Andrea.

   • Do you think the movie star would be able to successfully sue Andrea for defamation? Explain why or why not.

3. Suppose that Bob, who is neither rich nor famous, makes some neighbors angry. One of those neighbors posts a statement on her web site that says that Bob was fired for being late for work a lot. Unfortunately, although this embarrasses Bob, it is also true—Bob was fired for showing up late for work too often.

   • Explain why Bob would not be able to successfully sue his neighbor for defamation.

   • Because Bob cannot sue his neighbor for defamation, and defamation is not a crime, does that mean that what the neighbor did was okay? Explain why or why not.

4. Do you think that the increasing use of the Internet is going to cause more lawsuits for defamation in the future? Explain why or why not.

Downloading, Part I -------------------------------------

THE RECORDING INDUSTRY reported a decrease in sales of CDs in 2002 from 2001. The industry also experienced a decrease in sales in 2001 from the previous years. One reason for these two years of declining sales was the United States' economic recession. Some people had less money available to spend on discretionary items, such as music. (A *discretionary item* is something that one does not have to buy, as opposed to necessities like food and housing.)

However, beyond economic reasons, the recording industry places most of the blame for declining sales on the illegal downloading of music on the Internet. In May 2002, researchers conducted a survey for the Recording Industry Association of America (RIAA). This survey of 860 Internet-connected music consumers ages twelve to fifty-four found that by more than a two-to-one margin, people who say they are downloading more music from the Internet also say they are purchasing fewer CDs. Overall, the RIAA claims that the recording industry is losing over $4.2 billion a year to piracy activities, such as illegal downloading.

Music is not the only entertainment form that is illegally distributed through the Internet. The Motion Picture Association of America (MPAA) estimates that the United States motion picture industry loses in excess of $3 billion annually in potential worldwide revenue due to piracy. Most of this piracy occurs through activities such as selling illegal copies of videos and DVDs. In fact, the MPAA says that because it is so difficult to determine how much piracy takes place on the Internet, those figures are not included in the Association's current loss estimates. However, the MPAA points to Internet piracy of movies as a growing trend. Jack Valenti, president of the MPAA, estimates that 400,000 to 600,000 copies of films are illegally traded every day.

Some people acknowledge that illegally downloading music and movies is wrong and costs music and film companies money. However, many of these people say that these industries are still making plenty of money each year.

Record your answers below. Use another sheet of paper, if necessary.

1. Do you believe that the fact that music and film companies are selling billions of dollars worth of CDs, DVDs and videos makes it okay to illegally download music and movies, or not? Explain why you answered the way you did.

2. Do you think the fact that recording companies are experiencing decreasing sales makes it more likely or less likely that they will sign new musicians to recording contracts? Explain why you answered the way you did.

(continued)

Downloading, Part I -

3. Do you think the fact that film studios are experiencing lost sales makes it more likely or less likely that they will encourage new movie directors and actors to enter the film industry? Explain why you answered the way you did.

Some people who support downloading music and movies from the Internet argue that it is not really illegal. They point out that most of the downloading occurs on web sites that allow "peer to peer file sharing." This means that people get on-line and upload some of the music and movies they have to share with others. They compare this to having a book and giving it to a friend to read, which is perfectly legal. Those who criticize file sharing on the Internet say that it ultimately hurts the people who work for the recording companies, music stores, film studios, theater and rental chains, as well as the musicians and actors themselves. They also point out that there is a big difference between loaning one book and uploading a song that can be downloaded thousands of times.

4. Regardless of how you personally feel about the subject of illegal downloading, list and describe three reasons why it is a bad thing.

5. Regardless of how you personally feel about the subject of downloading, list and describe three reasons why it is a good thing.

6. Imagine that you are an executive at one of the big music or film companies. What would you do to combat illegal downloading of your company's music or movies? Explain why you answered the way you did.

Downloading, Part II -

IN FEBRUARY 2003, the Recording Industry Association of America (RIAA) and Motion Picture Association of America (MPAA) got together and sent a brochure to the largest 1,000 companies in the United States. The brochure warned those companies that some employees of those companies might be using the companies' computers to illegally download movies and music for their own use.

Record your answers below. Use another sheet of paper, if necessary.

Download the RIAA/MPAA Brochure from this web site:
www.riaa.com/news/newsletter/pdf/brochure2003.pdf

Read the brochure, and then answer the following questions.

1. If you were an executive at one of the 1,000 corporations that received the brochure, how would you feel about receiving this brochure? Explain your answer.

2. List three reasons the brochure provides to corporate leaders for supervising their employees' use of computers.

3. Imagine that you are an executive at a large corporation. You find out that several employees are using the company's computers to illegally download movies or music during their working hours. What action would you take regarding those employees? Explain your answer.

4. The brochure refers to a "compliance officer." Explain what you think is the job of a compliance officer.
   - Would you want to be a compliance officer at a company? Explain why or why not.

Downloading, Part III -

MANY SCHOOLS AND COLLEGES are concerned that students are using their Internet connections to illegally download music and movies. Some schools have begun campaigns to discourage students from downloading. Part of the problem that schools face is that students do not like to be preached at by teachers and other older adults on this subject. Therefore, some schools are relying instead on students to get the message out. These schools have asked students to create web sites, posters, and other media to encourage students to obey the law.

Record your answers below. Use another sheet of paper, if necessary.

1. Do you think that students are better able to discourage illegal downloading than teachers and other older adults? Explain why or why not.

2. In the space below, create a poster or the layout of a web page designed to discourage students at your school from illegally downloading music. Use your creativity—there is no single best way to get the message out.

For an example of one college's campaign against illegal downloading, visit the University of Delaware's "Code of the Web" site: www.udel.edu/codeoftheweb/.

Buying a Car -

MANY PEOPLE SAY that we will spend more money over our lifetime on cars than we will on housing. This is because a home can last forever, whereas a car needs frequent servicing and has to be replaced every few years. As a result, buying a car is one of the more important decisions a person has to make.

If you are a teenager, chances are that you are interested in getting a car of your own, if you do not already have one. And chances are that even though you would love your very own Escalade or tricked-out Civic, you do not have enough money (yet!) to buy the car of your dreams. Regardless of what your current car ownership status is, in this activity we will imagine that you have approximately $9,000 to $10,000 available for a car, and that you are going to use the Internet to research the cars that are available in that price range.

Answer the following questions. Use another sheet of paper, if necessary.

1. Before you begin your Internet search, write three important items of information that you will need to know about cars that are available for $10,000. For each item, explain why it is important.

2. Before you begin your Internet search, write the name of the web site that you think is the best place to begin your search, and explain why.

3. Okay, now it is time to begin searching on the web. As you do so, record your search as a flowchart. On a sheet of paper, draw a box for each web site you visit. In the box, write down the name of each site you visit and what information you found there. Not all sites will be helpful, as some will not have useful information, and some will only repeat information you have already found. If this is the case, simply write that you found no useful information below the name of the site. For each site you visit, draw an arrow to the next site you visit. If you go back and forth between sites, draw a two-sided arrow (↔). Continue surfing the Web and recording your research in the flowchart until you believe that you have found just the car you want.

(continued)

Buying a Car -----------------------------------

Example:

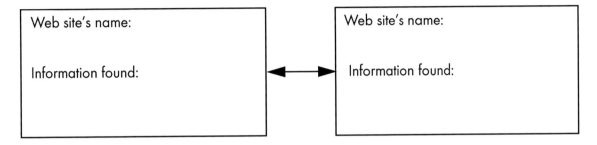

Web site's name:

Information found:

Web site's name:

Information found:

4. After completing your search, write a summary of what you learned. In your summary, include a discussion of each of the following:

- What car did you decide on?

- Why did you decide on that car?

- Did you find the type of car that you thought you wanted before beginning your search, or did you find a different type of car? Explain your answer.

- What was the most encouraging part of your search? Explain why.

- What was the most discouraging part of your search? Explain why.

- If you were really searching for a car (rather than doing this activity), would you use the Internet to help you search? Explain why or why not.

Choosing a College, Choosing a Career - - - - - - - - - - - - - - - -

AS A TEENAGER, you have probably begun to consider what you want to do after high school. Many teenagers go to college. However, not everybody wants to go to college. Even some of those who plan to go to college eventually want to do something else in the meantime.

This activity asks you to use the Internet to investigate the choices that are available to you after high school.

For each of the following questions that does not apply to you, simply write n/a, which stands for "not applicable."

Record your answers below. Use another sheet of paper, if necessary.

1. If you are planning to go to college, explain why. (Then skip to question 4.)

2. If you are planning never to go to college, explain why. (Then skip to question 5.)

3. If you think you might go to college after doing something else for a while, explain why. (Then go on to question 4.)

4. This question is for those thinking about going to college. You already know that college is an expensive undertaking that strains the budgets of most families. Of course, most people view this expense as a necessary and important one. Some studies find that college graduates make an average of $1 million more during their careers than non-college graduates do.

   • Think about some of the colleges you may be interested in attending. How much does tuition cost at those schools?

   • If you do not know, where do you think you would look on the Internet to find out?

   • How do you think you will pay for college? Explain.

   • Skip to question 6.

(continued)

Choosing a College, Choosing a Career - - - - - - - - - - - - -

5. Of course, college is not for everybody. Life is not just about money. Moreover, many plumbers, carpenters, and hair stylists make much more money than teachers or other college-educated people do. More importantly, many people *enjoy* jobs that do not require college. If you are not seriously considering college at this time, what careers are you thinking about instead? Explain.

- What training or skills do you need for those careers? If you do not know, where do you think you would look on the Internet to find out?

- Where does one obtain the training or skills needed for those careers? If you do not know, where do you think you would look on the Internet to find out?

- Do you know what the average salary is for those careers? If not, where do you think you would look on the Internet to find out?

- Go on to question 6.

6. Visit the "Mapping Your Future" web site (www.mapping-your-future.org/MHSS/), and investigate your options for life after high school. Write your conclusions about what you found at this web site.

For Whom Do I Vote? -

IN ACTIVITY 5 in Unit 2, we discussed whether Internet voting in political elections was a good idea or not. That activity focused on broad social issues. Here we focus on how you would make decisions about the candidate for whom you would vote. Teenagers are able to vote once they reach the age of eighteen. However, it is probably a good idea to have some knowledge of the issues before it is time to actually vote.

Choose a political election that is coming up in the near future. It may be a presidential election, which is held every four years (2004, 2008, and 2012). Most presidential candidates' web sites are posted on the Internet more than a year before the election. It may be an election for governor (a gubernatorial election) of your state. The year of gubernatorial elections vary from state to state. Your teacher will be able to help you identify an upcoming election if you need help. Most serious candidates for political office today maintain campaign web sites. Use a search engine, such as Google (www.google.com) or Ask Jeeves (www.ask.com), to find the web sites for the candidates.

Answer the following questions. Use another sheet of paper, if necessary.

1. Identify two candidates who are running against each other for the same political office. Visit the web site of each candidate. For each candidate, answer the following questions.

Candidate 1	Candidate 2
1. Name of candidate:	1. Name of candidate:
2. Office candidate is running for (president, governor, and so forth):	2. Office candidate is running for (president, governor, and so forth):
3. Political party of candidate (Democratic, Republican, and so forth):	3. Political party of candidate (Democratic, Republican, and so forth):
4. Candidate's age:	4. Candidate's age:
5. Candidate's education:	5. Candidate's education:
6. Candidate's political experience, if any:	6. Candidate's political experience, if any:
7. Candidate's position on standardized testing for high school students (If it is available on the candidate's web site. This is a hot topic, so you are likely to find something mentioned):	7. Candidate's position on standardized testing for high school students (If it is available on the candidate's web site. This is a hot topic, so you are likely to find something mentioned):

(continued)

Activity 10 *(continued)*

For Whom Do I Vote? --------------------------------

Candidate 1	Candidate 2
8. Candidate's position on abortion, if given: 9. A question of *your own* on the candidate's position—search for a topic that is important *to you:*	8. Candidate's position on abortion, if given: 9. A question of *your own* on the candidate's position—search for a topic that is important *to you:*

2. What important information, if any, were you *not* able to find at a candidate's web site?

3. If you could not find important information at the candidate's web site, where else would you look on the Internet for this information?

4. Continue to browse through each candidate's web site. If you were going to vote in the election in question, which candidate would you vote for? Explain why. (If you would vote for neither candidate, write that. Explain why.)

5. If voting in other elections in the future, would you use the Internet to help you make decisions about whom to vote for? Explain why or why not.

The FBI's Carnivore -

IN 2000, the Federal Bureau of Investigation (FBI) began using an Internet surveillance technology that it calls *Carnivore*. Carnivore is able to "sniff" people's e-mail, as it searches for evidence of crimes that the FBI is investigating. Carnivore can identify certain key words in e-mail messages as the FBI searches for evidence of criminal conspiracies, terrorism, and other serious crimes.

Record your answers below. Use another sheet of paper, if necessary.

1. Many politicians and other law-abiding members of the public were very concerned when Carnivore first began operating. Why do you think that some people who are not criminals were afraid of Carnivore? Explain your answer.

2. Soon after the introduction of Carnivore, the FBI said it regretted the name chosen for this new technology. Why do you think the Bureau regretted the name? Explain your answer.

3. As stated above, many people expressed concern about Carnivore when it began operating in 2000. However, after the attacks of September 11, 2001, a lot of people's attitudes about Carnivore changed. Explain why you think this happened.

4. Are you personally concerned about the FBI's ability to look through people's e-mail? Explain why or why not.

5. Would your answer to question 4 have been different *before* September 11, 2001? Explain why or why not.

6. What restrictions, if any, would you place on the FBI's ability to look through people's e-mail? (You may want to consider length of time of surveillance, types of crimes that are suspected, what the FBI does with the information it collects, and other issues.)

Want to know more about Carnivore? Visit computer.howstuffworks.com/carnivore.htm.

Glossary

click-through—an advertisement on the Internet that, if clicked on, takes the viewer to a web site at which the viewer can get more information about the product or perhaps make an on-line purchase of that product.

cookie—a unique identifier put on your computer by web sites when you surf the Internet. That cookie identifies you to the web site when you return to it, or to other web sites that share cookies with each other.

demographics—statistics about people grouped by such information as age, gender, ethnicity, geography, and income. For example, we know that the demographic group that buys the most individual sized packages of snack food is between the ages of twelve and twenty-four.

interactivity—the ability of people on both sides of a message to communicate with each other. The telephone and the Internet both allow interactivity; television does not.

ISP—short for Internet Service Provider. This company provides Internet access to a home, a school, or an office. Some of the more popular ISPs include AOL, MSN, and Earthlink. ISPs provide their service through telephone dial-up, broadband cable, or DSL (Digital Subscriber Line, available through telephone companies).

portal—a web site that is often used by consumers as their start page. Such portals include Yahoo and MSN. Portals offer content that is interesting to web surfers, which helps those portals gather viewers. The portals then can make money by selling advertising space to advertisers who want to sell products or services to those web surfers.

psychographics—information about people grouped by their interests, attitudes, values, and habits (including buying habits).

search engine—a web site designed to help people find information on the Internet. Examples include Excite (www.excite.com) and Google (www.google.com).

software—the programs in a computer that allow a computer to operate (system software) and provide different uses for the computer (application software). An example of system software is Microsoft's Windows. An example of application software is Corel's WordPerfect.

target market—the demographic or psychographic group (see definitions above) that the producers of a television show and its advertising sponsors want to reach. For example, a beer company may want male viewers to see its advertisements, so it advertises during football games, when men are most likely to be watching.

URL—uniform resource locator. This is the technical term for a web site address. URLs begin with http:// (which stands for hypertext transfer protocol), often followed by www (for World Wide Web). Because some URLs seem more logical to somebody who is trying to guess an address for a type of product, some URLs are considered very valuable. For example, www.cooking.com is, predictably, a web site that sells cooking equipment.

(continued)

Additional Resources

Publications

Blood, Rebecca, *The Weblog Handbook* (Cambridge, Mass.: Perseus, 2002).

Cozic, Charles P., ed., *The Future of the Internet* (San Diego: Greenhaven, 1997).

Gilster, Paul, *Digital Literacy* (New York: Wiley Computer Pub., 1997).

Goranson, Christopher D., *Everything You Need to Know About Misinformation on the Internet* (New York: Rosen, 2002).

Jones, Steve, ed., *Doing Internet Research* (Thousand Oaks, Calif.: Sage, 1999).

Mintz, Anne P., ed., *Web of Deception* (Medford, N.J.: CyberAge Books, 2002).

Web Sites

Bibliography for Evaluating Web Information
www.lib.vt.edu/research/evaluate/evalbiblio.html

Electronic Privacy Information Center
www.epic.org

Federal Trade Commission's Kids Privacy
www.ftc.gov/kidzprivacy

Internet Safety Education Foundation
www.isafe.org

Mapping Your Future
www.mapping-your-future.org

National Consumer League's Internet Fraud Tips
www.fraud.org/internet/intinfo.htm

Pew Internet and American Life
www.pewinternet.org

UCLA Center for Communication Policy Internet Project
www.ccp.ucla.edu/pages/InternetStudy.asp

U.S. Department of Energy CIAC Hoaxbusters
hoaxbusters.ciac.org

Usable Web Design Tips
usableweb.org/topics/000445-0-0.html

Share Your Bright Ideas

We want to hear from you!

Your name_____Date_____

School name_____

School address_____

City _____State _____Zip_____Phone number (_____)_____

Grade level(s) taught_____Subject area(s) taught_____

Where did you purchase this publication?_____

In what month do you purchase a majority of your supplements?_____

What moneys were used to purchase this product?

_____School supplemental budget   _____Federal/state funding   _____Personal

Please "grade" this Walch publication in the following areas:

	A	B	C	D
Quality of service you received when purchasing	A	B	C	D
Ease of use	A	B	C	D
Quality of content	A	B	C	D
Page layout	A	B	C	D
Organization of material	A	B	C	D
Suitability for grade level	A	B	C	D
Instructional value	A	B	C	D

COMMENTS:_____

_____

What specific supplemental materials would help you meet your current—or future—instructional needs?

_____

Have you used other Walch publications? If so, which ones?_____

May we use your comments in upcoming communications?   _____Yes   _____No

Please **FAX** this completed form to **888-991-5755**, or mail it to

Customer Service, Walch Publishing, P. O. Box 658, Portland, ME 04104-0658

We will send you a **FREE GIFT** in appreciation of your feedback. **THANK YOU!**